Giving
to
God

Biblical Principles of
Stewardship

DR. DAVID JEREMIAH

with Dr. David Jeremiah

Contents

About
Dr. David Jeremiah
and Turning Point

D r. David Jeremiah is the founder of Turning Point, a ministry committed to providing Christians with sound Bible teaching relevant to today's changing times through radio broadcasts, audiocassette series, and books. Dr. Jeremiah's "common sense" teaching on topics such as family, stress, the New Age, angels, and biblical prophecy forms the foundation of Turning Point.

Dr. Jeremiah is the senior pastor of Shadow Mountain Community Church in El Cajon near San Diego, California, where he also serves as president of Christian Heritage College. He and his wife, Donna, have four children.

In 1982, Dr. Jeremiah brought the same solid teaching to San Diego television that he shares weekly with his congregation. Shortly thereafter, Turning Point expanded its ministry to radio. Dr. Jeremiah's inspiring messages are currently broadcast weekly from more than 300 national and international radio stations.

Because Dr. Jeremiah desires to know his listening audience, he travels nationwide holding "A Night of Encouragement" radio rallies and Spiritual Enrichment conferences that touch the hearts and lives of many. According to Dr. Jeremiah, "At some point in time, everyone reaches a turning point, and for every person that moment is unique, an experience to hold onto forever. There's so much changing in today's world that sometimes it's difficult to choose the right path. Turning Point offers people an under-standing of God's Word, as well as the opportunity to make a difference in their lives."

Dr. Jeremiah has authored numerous books including *Escape the Coming Night* (Revelation), *The Handwriting on the Wall* (Daniel), *Turning Toward Joy* (Philippians), *Turning Toward Integrity* (James), *Invasion of Other Gods* (New Age), *Overcoming Loneliness, What the Bible Says About Angels, The Power of Encouragement,* and *Prayer—The Great Adventure.*

About This Study Guide

The purpose of this Turning Point study guide is to reinforce Dr. David Jeremiah's dynamic, in-depth teaching on stewardship and to aid the reader in applying biblical truth to his or her daily life. This study guide is designed to be used in conjunction with Dr. Jeremiah's *Giving to God* audiocassette series, but it may also be used by itself for personal or group Bible study.

Structure of the Lessons

Each lesson is based on one of the tapes in the *Giving to God* audiocassette series and focuses on a specific passage on stewardship. Each lesson is composed of the following elements:

• Outline

The outline at the beginning of the lesson gives a clear, concise picture of the passage being studied and provides a helpful framework for readers as they listen to Dr. Jeremiah's teaching.

• Overview

The overview summarizes Dr. Jeremiah's teaching on the passage being studied in the lesson. Readers should refer to the passage in their own Bibles as they study the overview.

• Application

This section contains a variety of questions designed to help readers dig deeper into the lesson and the Scriptures, and to apply the lesson to their daily lives. For Bible study groups or Sunday school classes, these questions will provide a springboard for group discussion and interaction.

• Did You Know?

This section presents a fun fact, historical note, or insight which adds a point of interest to the preceding lesson.

Using This Guide for Group Study

The lessons in this study guide are suitable for Sunday school classes, small-group studies, elective Bible studies, or home Bible study groups. Each person in the group should have his or her own study guide.

When possible, the study guide should be used with the corresponding tape series. You may wish to assign the study guide as homework prior to the meeting of the group and then use the meeting time to listen to the tape and discuss the lesson.

For Continuing Study

A complete catalog of Dr. Jeremiah's materials for personal and group study is available through Turning Point. To obtain a catalog, additional study guides, or more information about Turning Point, call 1-800-947-1993 or write to: Turning Point, P.O. Box 3838, San Diego, CA 92163.

Dr. Jeremiah's "Turning Point" radio broadcast is currently heard on more than 300 national and international radio stations. Contact your local Christian radio station or Turning Point for program times in your area.

Giving
to
God

A nd God is able to make all grace abound toward you, that you, always having all sufficiency in all things, have an abundance for every good work."

—2 Corinthians 9:8

Most people hate talking about their money. If you really want to make some people nervous, walk into a social gathering sometime and start asking questions about money. Immediately you'll see people clam up, stare at the floor, or simply sneak quietly away. Some people might start offering some advice about stewardship and investing, but if you ask them how well they follow their own advice, you'll get the same response. When it comes to money, there is always embarrassment, vague answers, and occasionally some anger that anyone would have the temerity to ask such personal questions.

But the fact is, with God there are no secrets. He knows how much we make. He knows how much we give. I don't know why we act like money is such a secretive thing, since one day each of us will stand before the Lord and be asked to give an accounting for all of the resources He has allowed us to have. It seems to me that we should take a hard look at finances—how we earn them, how we spend them, and how we use them for God's purposes. You see, everything we have is God-given. Any financial resources we are able to use came as a gracious gift from God. As a matter of fact, the investment of money in the New Testament is called a "grace." The word in the Greek is *charis*, and suggests beauty, health, and love. That's what our money ought to produce in the church. Giving should become an act of beauty, a statement of health, a reflection of love.

When we start thinking of stewardship in that way, our perspective of both giving and God changes. Giving becomes an exhilarating act of worship, not an obligatory exercise in church membership. We start to see God as the source behind all the needs as well as all the resources. And we recognize that the Bible promises the more we give, the more we have to give. God enhances our finances, rather than depleting them. We possess so that we may pass on.

We like to sing in church that "He is able, more than able, to accomplish what concerns me today." But if we really believe that, we will generously give to Him in order that He can use us to help change the world. The fact is, God is able. He waits only for enterprising men and women who will dare to believe Him. In this study we will begin to explore what the Bible has to say about sowing, stewardship, and sacrifice. As we come to understand the promises in God's Word regarding our finances, it will not only change our pattern of giving, but build our faith and revolutionize our perspective of God. As Paul put it in 2 Corinthians 9:10, "Now may He who supplies seed to the sower, and bread for food, supply and multiply the seed you have sown and increase the fruits of your righteousness."

My prayer, as you begin this study, is that the Spirit will move in your heart and change you, so that you can begin to participate in His plan for the ages.

MEET THE "STEWARD" OF STEWARDSHIP

G E N E S I S   2 4

Ve have all heard that we should be "good stewards," but what exactly is a steward? In this chapter, we will explore the concept of stewardship and four principles we need to keep in mind if we are to become stewards on God's behalf.

I. **Stewardship**
II. **Aspects of Stewardship**
    A. We do not own anything—God owns it all.
    B. Whatever we have is not ours, but His—we simply administer things on His behalf.
    C. How we administer what God has entrusted to us determines whether or not we can be given anything else.
    D. We shall all give an account someday.

We live in a world of financial bombardment where we face solicitations and appeals on almost a daily basis. How are we to respond to all the requests for funds? What do we do when faced with an appeal for our money? What principles has God given us to help us control what we do with our finances?

Many would say that we respond emotionally. Professional fund-raisers know that if they push the right emotional buttons, they can successfully solicit money. Certainly our emotions ought to be involved in our giving, but when we examine the multitude of opportunities brought before us, there must be a better way to decide what we'll distribute.

Stewardship

Fortunately, God has given us His wisdom. The Word of God speaks often about the concept of "stewardship," a much-talked-about word that most people do not understand. "Stewardship" is a concept that goes way beyond spending money—in fact, the use of money is a very small part of what it means to be a steward. In New Testament Greek, the word *steward* referred to either a slave or free man who was given household responsibilities, either as guardian of children or administrator of affairs. Every household of wealth and distinction had a steward, and he was in charge of the estate, often functioning as the manager of financial affairs and holdings.

The Hebrew word translated "steward" in the Old Testament was *ben-meshach*, which literally means "son of acquisition." In Genesis 15:2, Abraham uses the word to refer to Eliezer as the "steward" or "heir" of his house. Eliezer, the trusted steward, was the one who represented Abraham in all of his dealings. That's why, in Genesis 24, Abraham gave Eliezer the assignment to find a wife for Abraham's son, Isaac. A careful reading of that chapter reveals several important insights regarding the work of a steward.

First, notice that the steward was **accountable** for his master's domain. In verse 2 of chapter 24, Eliezer is described as the servant "who ruled over all that he had." Eliezer was responsible for everything that belonged to Abraham. In verse 10 we read that the servant took ten camels from the herds, "for all his master's goods were in his hand." Eliezer had authority over Abraham's herds, but with that authority came accountability.

Second, the steward was **available** when his master needed him. When Abraham called Eliezer to give him a special assignment, the servant was at his master's disposal. As the steward, Eliezer was to do whatever the master required of him.

Third, note that the steward was **anxious to know** the master's will. When he was given the assignment to go into the far country and find a wife for Isaac, Eliezer requested additional information. He wanted to make sure he got the right woman! He talked it over with Abraham, to make sure he had the will of his master in his own heart. It is important to keep that principle in mind, for when God gives us something to do, He is never offended when we come to request more information in order to obey Him well.

Fourth, the steward was **allegiant** to his master. Verse 9 tells us that Eliezer "put his hand under the thigh of Abraham his master, and swore to him concerning this matter." Of course, the servant was committed to his master already, but no one who is committed will be offended when asked to affirm his commitment. Occasionally I have had people in churches complain that they don't like writing out "commitment cards," but my experience has shown me that people who don't like to affirm their commitments usually are not committed! If I am committed to my master, I'll happily affirm it. So Abraham's servant eagerly agreed to commit himself anew to this particular assignment.

Fifth, it is clear that the steward was **agreeable** to his master's bidding. Verses 12-14 record Eliezer's prayer, in which he asks for guidance and grace in fulfilling his master's desires. A true steward not only administrates the affairs of another, he does it with a deep desire to reflect his master's will.

Finally, the steward **attributed praise** to his master. In verse 35, after locating the family of Isaac's future bride, Eliezer spoke of the greatness of his master, and you can sense the pride and excitement in his words. He was thrilled to be able to faithfully serve Abraham, and he wanted to tell his new friends about the greatness of his master. Eliezer is the kind of steward every business owner wants to find—one who will manage the business on the owner's behalf, while reflecting the owner's heart.

Aspects of Stewardship

Eliezer is just one example of an Old Testament steward, managing things on the owner's behalf. Jacob was also a steward, managing Laban's flocks and herds for seven long years in order to marry his daughter. Joseph was another steward who took charge of his master's domain. Though unjustly sold as a slave by his brothers, Joseph came to administrate the entire affairs of Potiphar, and later the affairs of all Egypt. Genesis 39:4 tells us that Potiphar made Joseph "overseer of his house, and all that he had." That's why, when faced with temptation at the hands of Potiphar's wife, Joseph replied, "My master does not know what is with me in the house, and he has committed all that he has to my hand. There is no one greater in this house than I, nor has he kept back anything from me but you, because you are his wife. How then can I do this great wickedness and sin against God?" Joseph recognized that his master had given him complete control, and his job was to please the will of his master.

There are two words translated "steward" in the New Testament that add another aspect to our understanding of stewardship. In Galatians 4:1-2 we read that "a slave, though he is master of all . . . is under guardians and stewards until the time appointed by the father." The King James translates that as "guardians and tutors." A tutor looks after someone's children on behalf of the parents. A guardian looks after their affairs or household. Both of these words can also be translated "steward," and refer to the act of taking care of something that belongs to another.

Jesus often used the concept of stewardship in his parables. For instance, in the parable of the laborers recorded in Matthew 20, the owner of the vineyard puts his steward in charge of the labor force, telling him to pay the workers whatever they have earned. The steward manages the laborers on behalf of his master. In the parable of the pounds in Luke 19, the parable of the talents in Matthew 25, and the parable of the wicked vinedressers in Matthew 21, a steward manages responsibilities on behalf of someone else.

Christ used this same concept when he assigned responsibilities to his disciples. "Who then is that faithful and wise steward, whom his master will make ruler over his household, to give them their portion of food in due season?" the Lord asks in Luke 12:42. He was gathering his followers in order to say, "I am getting ready to go back to heaven, and I am now putting you in charge." The Apostle Paul continued that thought when he wrote in Titus 1:7 that a bishop must be "blameless, as a steward of God." That verse reveals that churches don't belong to pastors—they belong to God. The pastor's role is to be a good steward of God's people, for one day he'll have to make an accounting.

Remember, then, that stewardship is not a matter of coming to church in order to give God 10% of your income and keep the other 90% as your own. As stewards, all 100% belongs to God, and one day when we stand before Him, we'll have to give an account of what we've done with His resources. We won't simply be asked to explain what we did with 10%, but be held responsible for everything He has put into our hands. Stewardship is a lofty and dignified principle, not a gimmick for getting money into the offering plates of churches. It is God's method for running things here on earth, and He has given us the blessed opportunity to be part of it. With that in mind, let's look at the following five principles.

We do not own anything—God owns it all.

If someone says to you, "Come see my house," what they're really inviting you to see is the house God gave them to manage. If someone invites you to drive their new car, what they're really inviting you to drive is God's car—though He is allowing them to drive it for awhile. If someone extols the virtues of their business, what they are really praising is the Lord. It's God's business, but He arranges for someone to manage it on His behalf. In case you don't believe that, consider these verses:

> Leviticus 25:23: "The land is Mine."
> Psalm 24:1: "The earth is the Lord's."
> Psalm 50:10: "For every beast of the forest is Mine."
> Haggai 2:8: "The silver is Mine, and the gold is Mine."
> Ezekiel 18:4: "All souls are Mine."
> 1 Corinthians 6:19-20: "You are not your own . . . you were bought at a price."

Every individual belongs to God. Everything we have belongs to God. Everything we claim is ours actually is owned by God. Therefore, never lose sleep over losing anything, because we own nothing. We are simply allowed to manage God's things for a short while.

Whatever we have is not ours, but His—we simply administer things on His behalf.

James 1:17 tells us that every good and perfect gift comes from the Father. It isn't something we have earned, but something He decides to give. That's why Deuteronomy 8:18 warns us to remember the Lord, "for it is He who gives you power to get wealth." A businessman may think he is a self-made man, but the very power to succeed came from God. As Paul said in 1 Timothy 6:7, 17, "For we brought nothing into this world, and it is certain we can carry nothing out . . . [it is] God who gives us richly all things to enjoy."

After one of the greatest offerings in history, King David had to actually tell the people to stop giving because they had given so much. After he had received the offering, David prayed these words, recorded in 1 Chronicles 29:14: "For all things come from You, and of Your own we have given You." I love those words, for they remind me that anything I give to God is merely a giving back of His own abundant blessing. I'm simply giving back to God what He already owns. It's like recycling the blessing for the kingdom of God. Everything we think we own belongs to God, and we administrate it on His behalf.

How we administer what God has entrusted to us determines whether or not we can be given anything else.

I've been in churches all my life, and I've heard countless sermons on stewardship. One of the popular images in the church is to say that "you can't out-give God." I once heard a pastor say that giving was like having a shovel, in which we give as much as possible to God, and He shovels it all right back to us. And since His shovel is bigger than ours, we always get back more than we gave. The problem with that illustration is that it brings God down to the level of "blessed bargainer." The Lord doesn't work that way.

God owns everything and has decided to put some of it into our hands to manage. When the Lord looks down and sees an individual doing a good job administering a few things, He decides to put that individual in charge of a few more things. God evaluates our stewardship on the basis of how well we administer it, keeping His priorities in mind rather than our own. When He sees someone serving faithfully, He expands the responsibility, giving something else to be managed. But when He sees someone who manages God's resources based on his own agenda, or who forgets to reflect the Spirit of God in his management, the Lord can choose to withhold any further responsibility.

That's why Jesus, in explaining the parable of the talents in Matthew 25:21, said, "Well done, good and faithful servant; you were faithful over a few things, I will make you ruler over many things." Another time, in Luke 16:10-11, the Lord noted, "He who is faithful in what is least is faithful also in much; and he who is unjust in what is least is unjust also in much. Therefore if you have not been faithful in the unrighteous mammon, who will commit to your trust the true riches?"

Occasionally I'll hear someone say, "I can't afford to tithe right now, but as soon as I get my next raise, I'm going to start giving to God." That person is deluding himself. If we cannot manage the little God has given us, we won't be able to manage more. And if we can't take care of the small things, God won't be interested in turning the big things over to us. Getting more responsibility would just make us more unfaithful as stewards. But when we prove ourselves faithful in the things God has given us, then He can entrust us with additional responsibilities.

We shall all give an account someday.

When Paul wrote to the Romans, he told them in 14:12 that "each of us shall give account of himself to God." We will have to "settle up" with the Lord some day. That's why 2 Corinthians 5:10 reminds us that "we must all appear before the judgment seat of Christ, that each one may receive the things done in the body, according to what he has done, whether good or bad." God owns everything, He entrusts to each of us a portion of what He owns so that we can manage it, and someday we'll each have to give an accounting for our actions. As stewards, we should expect nothing less.

The great preacher John Broadus once taught the members of his congregation a lesson on stewardship. As the ushers took up the offering, he walked up and down the aisles, looking at every penny and nickel put into the plate by his parishioners. As you can imagine, some of the people in church that day were furious, others were shamefaced, and everyone was surprised. But when Broadus walked back to his pulpit, he told his people that if they were upset that he had seen exactly what they had and had not given that day, they should remember that Jesus Christ, God's Son, walks the aisles with the ushers every Sunday. The Savior knows who is a faithful steward and who is not.

We do everything we can in our modern churches to protect the anonymity of the stewards. As a pastor, I don't know what anyone gives, nor do I want to know. But God knows exactly what we are doing with everything entrusted to our care, and one day we will have to account for all of it. What a thrilling thought it is to know that God has given us an opportunity to take care of His things! Let us make sure we are good stewards of His things.

APPLICATION   G E N E S I S   2 4

1. In what ways are you a steward at work? At school? At home?

What financial responsibilities do you have in your life?

What financial pressures do you feel in your life?

2. How do you define stewardship?

In Genesis 24, what was Eliezer responsible for?

How would you describe his attitude?

How did Eliezer's actions reflect his attitude?

3. Why is availability an essential ingredient to stewardship?

Why is it important to know the master's will?

How can a steward of God know His will?

4. What principles for stewardship do you find in the following passages:

>   Deuteronomy 8:18
>
>   1 Chronicles 29:14
>
>   Matthew 25:21
>
>   Luke 12:42
>
>   Galatians 4:1-2
>
>   1 Timothy 6:7, 17
>
>   James 1:17

What does it mean to you when you hear the words, "God owns everything"? Why is that important?

How is good stewardship tied to increased responsibility?

What would you say to someone who argued, "I already tithe ten percent—I don't have to give any more!"

What does Romans 14:12 have to say about our future responsibility to the Lord?

What lesson does 2 Corinthians 5:10 add to that teaching?

Why will each of us be called to give an accounting before the Lord?

Where do you find yourself struggling with money? Why?

When do you find it hardest to be a good steward?

When do you find it easiest?

The Greek word for "steward" is *oikonomos*. It was commonly used to describe the individual who managed the household and staff, but it was also used as a title for a city's treasurer. Since it usually was connected to someone in charge of finances, that Greek term has developed into the modern English word *economy*.

THE SERMON ON THE AMOUNT

OUTLINE   MALACHI 3 : 1 0 - 1 4

Nearly every Christian, at one time or another, has wondered about the amount of giving. How much should we give? How much is enough? In this study, we will answer that question by looking at the principle of tithing and its importance to the overall plan of God.

  I.   Tithing was the Method of God
 II.   Tithing was a Matter of Priority with God
III.   Tithing was a Means of Proving God
 IV.   Tithing was a Means of Provision by God
  V.   Putting the Principle of Tithing to Work

I used to think that I shouldn't preach in church about finances, because it is such a personal issue between the individual and God. But the more I studied the Scriptures, the more I realized God had tremendous things to say about the stewardship of our time, talent, and treasures. As a pastor, it was my responsibility to declare the whole counsel of God. For you see, when we are confronted with the truth about how we use the Lord's resources, we begin to see how our attitudes about money influence every other aspect of our lives.

We all know that an organization unclear about finances is an organization in trouble. If a bank doesn't solve its financial problems, it will go bankrupt. If a government doesn't solve its financial problems, there will be economic chaos. If a marriage doesn't solve its financial problems, there will be contention and quarreling. And if a church doesn't solve its financial problems, learning to deal with the challenges facing every growing organization, it will have a hard time fulfilling its mission.

Fortunately, the Bible doesn't leave us in the dark about how we are to function as a church. In the Old Testament Book of Malachi, we find these words: "'Bring all the tithes into the storehouse, that there may be food in My house, and try Me now in this,' says the LORD of hosts, 'if I will not open for you the windows of heaven and pour out for you such blessing that there will not be room enough to receive it'" (Malachi 3:10). This verse describes how God dealt with His people in the Old Testament and how His program was financed. The people tithed to Him, and He in turn blessed them.

Tithing was the Method of God

For fifteen centuries between Moses and Jesus, the law of the tithe was in place. Whenever the Jews ignored this law, they got into difficulty as a nation. When the Prophet Malachi was writing, Israel was returning to her homeland from captivity, having been punished for disobedience to the Lord. One would think that the Jews, having suffered so greatly at the hands of the Babylonians, would be quick to obey God and serve Him, but the truth is they weren't back in the land long before they started to backslide again. All the lessons of captivity were soon forgotten as the nation slid back toward sin. A casual reading of Malachi's message provides a realistic look at Israel's spiritual life. Judah was spiritually sick, and one of the evidences of her sickness was that she had forsaken the law of the tithe commanded by God. This departure from obedience demonstrated the people's lack of faith in the Lord. They didn't trust God to take care of them, so they took things into their own hands and began to violate His laws.

God has always expected His people to tithe. A careful reading of the Bible reveals that the concept of tithing (that is, giving ten percent to the Lord) did not begin with the Law. It pre-dates Moses, so those who argue they don't have to tithe because they are not under the Law are mistaken. Tithing goes back at least as far as Abraham, for in Genesis 14 we read how Abraham, after rescuing Lot, met with Melchizedek, king of Salem, and paid tithes to the Lord. The Book of Hebrews reveals that Melchizedek was a type of Christ, so we have an early example of tithing—God's man paying tribute to the Lord by giving Him ten percent.

In Genesis 28 there is another example of tithing, as Jacob promised to give one-tenth of everything he had to the Lord. Of course, Jacob's promise was rather self-centered, since he was trying to bargain with God by saying, "Get me out of this mess and I'll do anything you ask!" But the concept of a tithe was clearly evident long before Moses was handed the Law.

Once the Law was received, there was actually a more complex system of tithing. The Jews who lived in Israel under the Law were responsible for giving three different tithes. First, there was **the Lord's tithe**, described in Leviticus 27:30 & 32: "And all the tithe of the land, whether of the seed of the land or of the fruit of the tree, is the Lord's. It is holy to the LORD. . . . And concerning the tithe of the herd or the flock, of whatever passes under the rod, the tenth one shall be holy to the LORD." This money was collected to help the nation, much like we pay taxes to our government. Our government doesn't give a stewardship sermon about how to pay taxes—it just takes taxes out of your pay. The Jews lived in a theocracy, with the government built around the principles of God, so the church collected the Lord's tithe which made it possible for the government to function.

A second tithe the Jews paid was **the Levites' tithe**, which was given to the priests from the tribe of Levi because they didn't have an inheritance in the Promised Land. The other tribes were to take care of them, so this tithe consisted of corn and oil and wine, and it took care of the preachers and singers and those who ministered in the Temple.

The third tithe was called **the charity tithe**, given every third year for caring for the widows, strangers, and those in need. Deuteronomy 14 gives the details of this tithe, and it is similar to the fellowship offerings many churches have to care for those in the body who are facing an immediate financial crisis.

Of course, it doesn't take a financial genius to figure out the Jews were responsible for giving more than ten percent of their income to the things of God. If the two yearly tithes were added together, and the third tithe were spread out over three years, the annual percentage would add up to about 23%.

However, that wasn't the end of giving. The Scriptures also speak of "offerings," which were gifts made to God **in addition to their tithes**. The people of Israel were expected to voluntarily give gifts to the Lord. Some scholars have estimated that between 40% and 60% of a man's annual income was returned to the Lord. This was God's method for running the church and the nation. The Prophet Malachi reveals that one of Isreal's problems was that the people were robbing God of His tithes and offerings. In refusing to trust God and surrender their tithes, they were turning their backs on His method.

Tithing was a Matter of Priority with God

Occasionally I'll hear someone claim that the people of the Old Testament had to give under compulsion, while those in New Testament times are somehow more "free" to give. But that comparison is false, for we are just as responsible to tithe as those living in Old Testament times. The fact is, the people living in Malachi's time were supposed to be giving as an expression of their love for God, and their tithe was to reflect that spirit. If they failed to give out of love, it revealed a lack of spiritual vitality in their lives.

For example, in Malachi 1:8 we read, "When you offer the blind as a sacrifice, is it not evil? And when you offer the lame and sick, is it not evil? Offer it then to your governor! Would he be pleased with you? Would he accept you favorably?" You see, the Jews were supposed to bring a healthy animal and offer it as a sacrifice to the Lord. But some people were looking around for their smallest, weakest animal, or they were offering God a sick or blind animal. They were giving God their leftovers, and it revealed a weak spirituality. So Malachi asks them, "Would you give that to the government?" Try handing the tax man a smaller portion than he deserves and see what it gets you! The government wants what it is due and won't settle for something else.

The Lord is the same way. That's why Malachi says, "Cursed be the deceiver who has in his flock a male, and takes a vow, but sacrifices to the Lord what is blemished" (1:14). A person should not come to God and offer Him the scraps. If we recognize God as King and Lord, we ought to be unwilling to give Him leftovers. We are to be committed to excellence in everything we do. He expects the best we have to offer, whether that is with our money, our worship services, or anything else we do in His name. I don't believe God is pleased with anyone who eschews excellence to offer Him something unprepared and unsacrificial.

In the Old Testament, the people brought their offerings to God and made it a matter of priority. As we come to Him, we are to do the same. That means we don't give God the change left over after we've bought everything we want, nor do we offer Him the time we have left after packing our schedules with our own motivations and ambitions. God doesn't seek the talents we have left over after all our efforts have been put toward our own selfish ends, nor does He desire a tip out of the income He has entrusted into our care. Tithing has always been a matter of priority to God, and it should still be a matter of priority in our own lives.

Tithing was a Means of Proving God

"Try [Prove (KJV)] Me now in this," God says in Malachi 3:10. The Lord wanted the people of Israel to prove Him, so that he could demonstrate that He was capable of caring for them. If the people would bring their tithes to Him, He would prove His provision. This wasn't striking a bargain with God. From the beginning of time there have always been schemers who have attempted to use their money to buy His favor. The final spark that lit the conflagration we know as the Protestant Reformation was Martin Luther's condemnation of the selling of indulgences—that is, the church "selling" to an individual the privilege of sinning. One fellow who sold indulgences, a man by the name of Johann Tetzel, used this poem as his sales tool: "Soon as the money in the coffer rings, a soul from purgatory springs." If the person would just pay enough money, he could get out of hell. Some people seem to think if they have enough money, they can buy God.

But the Lord has never been for sale. He isn't "proved" by buying His attention. Tithing doesn't equal a relationship with God. But by being obedient to His commands, we demonstrate our belief in Him. Malachi was encouraging the nation of Israel to tithe in order to show that they trusted in His ability to care for them. Their outward obedience was evidence of an inner commitment. So when we tithe, we create an opportunity for God to prove Himself.

Tithing was a Means of Provision by God

Not only did tithing prove that God was real and that He cared for them, but when the Jews gave, God provided for their needs. In my own life, we have practiced tithing ever since we were first married. We've sometimes had our financial struggles, as all married couples do, but as I look back over our life together, I see how God has met our needs. It has been an adventure to see the Lord provide for us as we have been faithful to Him.

"Try Me now in this," the Lord says in Malachi 3:10, "If I will not open for you the windows of heaven and pour out for you such blessing that there will not be room enough to receive it." So God will provide a special blessing to those who faithfully obey His command to tithe. Then the Lord goes on to say in the next verse, "I will rebuke the devourer for your sakes, so that he will not destroy the fruit of your ground, nor shall the vine fail to bear fruit for you in the field." In other words, He gets personally involved with our work and our success when we obey Him.

When God speaks of rebuking the devourer, He is reminding the Jews that He has many ways of caring for His people. The Lord doesn't just give to us; He also protects us from harm. There have been times when I've had to drive a car that, according to the principles of physics, probably shouldn't have moved at all. It shouldn't start, and once started it shouldn't have kept going! But I am confident that God, in His mercy, kept the car moving as long as we needed it, providing for our need and proving His faithfulness. Though I cannot explain it, I've seen the Lord apparently multiply money so that a small amount took care of all our needs. In fact, one of the surprises that comes to the person who tithes is the ability to administrate the affairs of a house with a small amount of money. God just continues to provide, which offers us not only a material blessing, but a spiritual blessing as well.

Putting the Principle of Tithing to Work

Again, some Christians will argue that we no longer live under the law of tithing. But consider this question: Can you think of one New Testament example in which Jesus Christ took an Old Testament principle and lowered the bar? No, in fact the Lord usually raised the standard: "You have heard that it was said . . . but I say to you" (Matthew 5:21, 22). Jesus constantly held people to a higher standard of performance. So those who want to discount the biblical concept of tithing simply want to justify a lower level of giving. But they won't find support for that in the teachings of Jesus Christ.

The Old Testament established certain standards for giving to God's work. The New Testament says that we are to give as God prospers us (1 Corinthians 16), but that is no excuse for giving Him less. We are reminded that we reap what we sow—if we sow sparingly, we shall also reap sparingly. While there isn't any specific amount given us in the New Testament, there are several examples that encourage us to give generously. In the story of the widow's mite, the aged widow gave all that she had—100%! Similarly, the rich young ruler was told to give all that he had to the poor—100%. In the early church, the Book of Acts tells us that the believers had all things in common, even selling their property and giving all the money to the church—100%. And in Christ's command to Zacchaeus, the tax collector was instructed to give half of his goods to the poor—that's 50%.

Many people seem to want a figure of how much to give, but more important than a number is an attitude of gratitude to God. Every Christian I know who is happy giving to God is involved in systematic stewardship, and they started with a commitment to give God at least a tithe. They most probably wondered how they could ever afford it. But by faith they obeyed the Lord, and watched as the Lord blessed them and provided for their needs. Their joy and commitment grew as they learned about the faith that comes from commitment.

What we do with our money reveals what we really believe in. If we claim to believe in education, for example, we'll set money aside to put ourselves through school. Our checkbooks reveal our priorities. So make the decision to begin the adventure of giving to God and to start tithing 10% to your local church. Then start watching to see what God does in your life.

<hr>

APPLICATION   M A L A C H I   3 : 1 0 - 1 4

1. In your own words, how are stewardship and spirituality linked?

What attitude should we maintain, according to Luke 16: 11-13?

It has been said that every Christian can offer the Lord time, talent, and treasure. In what ways are you giving each of those to God?

2. What does Ecclesiastes 3:17 say about the way we use our time on earth?

What principles for using time wisely can you glean from the following verses:

Psalm 39:4

Psalm 89:47

Psalm 90:12

Romans 13:11-12

1 Corinthians 4:19

2 Corinthians 6:2

James 4:15

Read Ephesians 5:16 and Colossians 4:5. How do we "redeem" time?

As you study Acts 20:24 and 2 Timothy 4:2-8, how would you describe Paul's perspective on time?

What do the following passages teach us about giving our talent to God:

Luke 16:10

Romans 12:3, 6

1 Corinthians 4:1-2, 7

1 Corinthians 7:7, 17

1 Corinthians 12:11, 14-31

Read Luke 19:11-27. What did the five-talent man do right, and what was his reward?

What did the one-talent man do wrong, and what was his reward?

What principles would you draw from this parable for your own life?

What talent do you have that God could use?

4. Does God care how we make our money? Why?

What principles for managing money do you get from reading the following passages:

Matthew 6:31-32

2 Corinthians 9:12

Ephesians 4:28

Philippians 4:19

1 Timothy 6:10, 17

James 1:17

What would you say is the purpose of our money?

Read Malachi 3:8-12. What is the problem with those who do not tithe?

What promise does the Lord make to those who tithe?

What would you say to someone who argued, "I don't have to tithe. That's an Old Testament law, and I don't live under the law"?

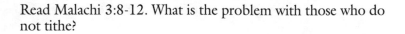

The Greek word translated "tithe" is *dekatoo*. It literally means "ten," which is why the ancients understood that to tithe meant to pay God one-tenth. The modern English word *decade* comes from *dekatoo*.

JESUS AT THE TREASURY

Jesus once sat in the Temple courtyard and watched an old woman surrender all she had to the Lord. As we examine her example, we find lessons for our own lives.

   I. **The Affluence from Which We Give**
  II. **The Amount That We Give**
 III. **The Appraisal of What We Give**
 IV. **The Lesson for What We Give**

33

A lfred Nobel was a Swedish chemist who made his fortune by inventing dynamite and other powerful explosive materials. Those materials, purchased by major governments around the world, were used to produce weapons of destruction. When Nobel's brother died, one newspaper printed Alfred's obituary by mistake. In it, Nobel was described as a man who became rich by enabling other people to kill each other in unprecedented numbers. When someone sent a copy to him, Alfred Nobel was so shaken by the assessment of his life that he resolved to use the fortune he had amassed to reward accomplishments that benefited humanity rather than destroy it. He established what we now know as "the Nobel Peace Prize."

Alfred Nobel had a rare opportunity. He was given the chance to see an evaluation of his life while he was still alive and able to change it. I sometimes wonder what each of us would do if we could have that same opportunity. What kind of epitaph would be on our gravestones if it were written today? And if we were given a chance to change things, to rewrite the obituary, how effective would we be at making changes?

The Bible is clear that God in heaven is watching carefully how we live. Like the children sing in Sunday School, "Be careful little hands what you do, for the Father up above is looking down in love." That is a truth from which we cannot escape, and which I continue to understand better. It is a truth which two great gospel singers, Mahalia Jackson and Ethel Waters, immortalized with the words, "His eye is on the sparrow, and I know He watches me." It is a great encouragement to know that no matter where I go or what I do, my heavenly Father is watching over me, understanding my needs, and caring for me. But there is another side to that: God is not only watching over my life for my protection; He is also watching over my life in order to evaluate it.

I've always thought it interesting that the last public act of Christ's ministry was neither a sermon nor a miracle, but an evaluation. Jesus visited Herod's Temple, sat down by the treasury, and watched what people gave to God. Our Lord spent the last day of his public ministry looking at an offering. "Jesus sat opposite the treasury and saw how the people put money into the treasury. And many who were rich put in much. Then one poor widow came and threw in two mites" (Mark 12:41-42).

There were thirteen treasuries in the courtyard of the Temple, each with a letter on it signifying the purpose of that particular treasury. Each one was shaped like a tall box, with a trumpet coming out of it much like that on the old RCA pictures. When a man cast money into it, it was possible to make the coins roll around, and be heard all over the Temple. Some people brought all their tithe in copper coins, so that they could walk up and throw it in, filling the courtyard with the sound of their gift. They gave so that they could be noticed. Jesus sat and watched these people as they walked by, dropping their coins into the boxes.

It should come as no surprise that Christ thought this action was important, for fully half His parables were devoted to the issue of money. Fifteen percent of everything He said recorded in Scripture has to do with our attitudes and actions with finances. Money, in one sense, is like life compressed. When we come to bring Him what we have earned, we are literally taking our lives and compressing them into the coinage of our day, saying, "Here is my life, God. Here are my hours and energy, melted down into coin. I give it to you." No Old Testament worshipper would have dreamed of coming to the house of God empty-handed. He understood the very essence of worship was to give back to God that which He had entrusted. The people wouldn't dream of coming into the Temple without first going to the treasury box and giving to the Lord. And if the Lord took the time to watch the treasury boxes in order to see how people worshipped in that comparatively poor culture, you can be sure He watches them now in our age of affluence.

Of course, what we do with our money is our own business. To allow someone else to watch us write out a check is uncomfortable, sometimes painful. But Jesus made it His business to know, and didn't apologize for watching the givers closely. He didn't have to, for His gaze is the only one that counts. In my church, it doesn't matter what I think about someone's giving pattern—it only matters what God thinks. The Bible says that Jesus went over deliberately and sat next to the treasuries, and He "beheld" them. The word *beheld* literally means gazed upon them as though they were a form of theater. He was close enough to see who threw in much and who tossed in little. The Lord even noticed the two small coins coming from the withered hand of a widow and created an object lesson for His disciples. He saw the crowds milling about, watching both rich and poor put in their offerings. Everybody came with something. And it makes me wonder, "What does God look for when He watches the treasury?"

The Affluence from Which We Give

Here was a contrast: one poor widow and many wealthy people. The Greek words describe that widow as being a pauper, one who must eke out a living each day. God knew all about that widow, and He knows all about each of us. He knows the circumstances from which we give. He knows if we have much or we have little.

Some people hide behind having much, but there are just as many who hide behind having little. If that widow were alive today, surely some Christians would tell her, "You're poor. God doesn't expect you to give anything when you have so little." It would be easy for me to stand up in church and tell those who are struggling financially that they no longer have to give, that the wealthy in the body would take care of the church's financial needs. But that's not how God designed the church. Our faith is revealed in our giving, whether we have much or little. The widow of Mark 12 didn't have much, but she didn't use that as an excuse not to give back to the Lord. She gave out of her poverty because she understood that God saw what she had. The Lord knows the affluence from which we give.

The Amount That We Give

The widow put in her two mites. The Greek word translated "mite" is actually *lepton*, and it was used to describe the smallest denomination of coin in the Greek world. A day's pay at that time was one denarius, and it took 128 leptons to make up one denarius. So you can see this widow barely had enough money to buy a scrap of bread. But she gave it all to the Lord. Even more interesting, she gave both coins, rather than keeping one for herself. Some might have encouraged her to keep one back in order to have something in reserve, but she surrendered them both to the Lord, trusting in Him completely.

I'm not sure many people today would understand the widow's thinking. We have a tendency to assume, "I have so little, surely God doesn't expect much of me." But God cares about the amount you give, so much that He took notice of the small change that was given by the widow in Mark 12. If He knows what she did with her money, we can count on the fact that He knows what we do with our money. Besides, if you made only $15,000 per year from the time you were 25 until you retired at 65, the Lord would expect you to give an account of more than half a million dollars. So perhaps it's time we stopped begging off on the basis that we have so little to share.

It's interesting that this widow became known for the amount she gave. Imagine if each of us were to be immortalized on the basis of how much (or how little) we contributed. Our offerings to God represent us. The two mites represented the widow, for she "put in more than all those who have given to the treasury" (Mark 12:43). She put in her entire life.

I heard a story recently about a pastor who made an appeal to his congregation for some worthy cause, and a woman handed him a check for $50. When she asked if her gift was enough, the pastor replied, "It's fine, if it represents you." After a moment's pause, she took back her check and wrote out a new one for $5,000. This time when she asked if it was enough, the pastor again replied, "Of course, if it represents you." Angry, the woman grabbed the check and walked away. But after several days of earnest prayer, that same woman handed a check for $50,000 to the pastor, saying, "This check represents me, and I'm happy to give it to the Lord." Remember, the Lord cares about the amount we give because it represents us.

The Appraisal of What We Give

It is interesting to see how the Lord evaluates the entire process of giving. God obviously invented mathematics and is the originator of numbers, so we have to remember that He understands the issue of finances better than anyone else. And as Jesus sat beside that treasury, watching rich and poor put money into it, "He called His disciples to Himself and said to them, 'Assuredly, I say to you that this poor widow has put in more than all those who have given to the treasury'" (Mark 12:43). Those words must have shaken up His disciples. They'd watched some wealthy people drop some pretty big gifts into the treasury, and then the Lord told them that the widow's two mites were worth more. It didn't make any sense to them, until He explained that "they all put in out of their abundance, but she out of her poverty put in all that she had, her whole livelihood" (v. 44).

The wealthy gave out of their surplus. The widow gave out of her life. The gifts given by the wealthy didn't touch life at all, but the widow's gift touched the very core of her being. You see, God doesn't evaluate our giving by what we give. He evaluates our giving by what we have. As Paul puts it in 2 Corinthians 8:12, "For if there is first a willing mind, it is accepted according to what one has, and not according to what he does not have." Interestingly, a study of philanthropy in America concluded that the people who make less than $10,000 per year give the greatest percentage of their income to the things of God. For every step up the income bracket, you'll find a smaller percentage of income being given away. The more a man makes, the less likely he is to give it away. The amount might be greater, but the percentage is actually smaller.

It seems a great irony that a poor man who walks with God and is rewarded with prosperity would gradually turn his attention away from the Lord. Yet history has shown that to be the case. Perhaps the economic prosperity our country has experienced is not a blessing, but a curse. Or, as a leader in the persecuted church of Romania once put it, "Ninety-five percent of the believers who face the test of persecution pass it, while 95% of those who face the test of prosperity fail it." That was certainly true of Israel. Whenever they were hungry and persecuted, they turned to the Lord. But whenever they experienced peace and prosperity, they turned toward evil. "They were filled and their heart was exalted," the Lord says in Hosea 13:6, "therefore they forgot Me." As a nation is blessed with more and more, they realize less and less the involvement of God.

The Lesson for What We Give

Physics tells us that the greater the mass, the greater the hold that mass exerts. That explains why the largest planets are capable of holding so many satellites in orbit. Similarly, the more things we own, the greater their mass, and the more they grip us. We think that we own things, but in reality things own us. They suck us in, until we become lost in our possessions, indistinguishable from the things we have, surrendering our humanity and sometimes our very souls.

When Jesus visited the treasury that day, He saw many people giving of their abundance, but He took note of one poor widow who gave to God all she had. When these two types of people are shown in contrast, we can better see the example we are to follow. The Bible often reveals two contrasting individuals to help us best see the truth. The generous Abraham is contrasted with the greedy Lot, and it was the generous man who succeeded. The big-hearted Barnabas, who sold property and gave the money to the early church, is contrasted with the self-centered actions of Ananias and Sapphira, who sold property but kept back some of the money. They wanted the applause and accolades accorded Barnabas, but God would not allow them to receive any glory for their actions. The unselfish Mary, who gave her alabaster box of perfume to anoint Jesus, is contrasted with the selfish Judas, who would have liked to get his hands on the money Mary spent on the Lord. The Scriptures often present the truth by revealing the contrast of two people.

When the Apostle Paul was taken in chains from a filthy Roman dungeon and beheaded at the order of a rich madman named Nero, there was a contrast between two representatives of humanity. One lived for prosperity on earth, the other for the riches of heaven. History remembers both men for what they were—one a saint, the other a scoundrel.

When we read about the widow in Mark 12, we see a woman who trusts completely in God, who gave everything she had to Him because she knew He would care for her. Perhaps if we were to examine our own hearts, we would find the reason we are reluctant to give is not so much a matter of treasure as it is a matter of trust. We have entrusted God with our eternal souls, but are unwilling to trust Him with our temporal riches.

I heard about a man who complained to his pastor about not having any money left over for God after paying his bills. The pastor asked him, "Would you be willing to trust God to take care of you, tithe every month, and bring me whatever bills you can't pay?" Of course the man quickly agreed to that plan, but that led the pastor to say, "It's strange you would trust me, an imperfect man, to care for your needs, but you will not trust Almighty God, who demonstrated His love for you by sending His Son to die on a cross." When it comes right down to it, we either trust God to take care of us, or we trust in our money. We either love Him, or we love money.

The widow at the Temple saw past the treasury box, past the poverty of her own life, and peered into eternity. She understood that the things worth living for are not in this world. The wealthy lived for this world, but the widow for the next. Every person is either moving toward the treasury or away from it. If we spend our life in pursuit of wealth, we waste it racing away from the true treasure of heaven. But the person whose treasures are locked away in eternity has every reason to rejoice, whether things in this life are easy or hard. For that person has learned to trust in the faithfulness of God, who is watching us as we approach the treasury.

APPLICATION   M A R K   1 2 : 4 1 - 4 4

1.   Why did Jesus sit beside the treasury?

What did He hope to see?

What was the difference in attitude between the wealthy and the widow?

In what ways could it be said the widow put in more than the wealthy?

How do you think the disciples responded to Christ's words in Mark 12:43?

Have you ever known anyone who gave everything to God? What were the circumstances?

What would you say to someone who complained, "I don't have much to give God"?

Does God know your financial state? Why does He allow varying degrees of wealth?

Why is it as important for a poor person as for a wealthy person to give to the Lord?

Is the amount of money we give to God important? Why or why not?

Why do you suppose a wealthy person generally gives a smaller percentage to charity than a person of modest means?

What do you suppose the Lord thinks of your giving pattern? Does it represent you?

What does 2 Corinthians 5:10 tell us about God's appraisal of our giving?

Why is it important that each of us will have to give an account?

If you were to write your epitaph, what would you want it to say? Why?

Why does wealth have a tendency to push us away from the Lord?

Have you ever felt that you were "owned" by your possessions, rather than owning them? When? What did you do to break out of that trap?

How can we keep our minds set on eternal treasures, rather than temporal ones?

7. When do you find it hardest to trust God?

What ministry or group have you always wanted to help financially?

What steps could you take right now to build your faith in Him?

The Jews developed a word for people who tossed their coins loudly into the treasury box in hopes of being noticed by others. These people were called "zingers," a name similar to the sound their coins made when they flung them into the trumpets at the top of the boxes.

DRAWING INTEREST

God's Word contains some important principles that ought to guide our giving. The Bible says we owe God our very lives, so out of love and obedience, we give back to Him some of what He has so graciously given to us. In this chapter we will explore three principles for drawing interest on the principle of God's Word.

    I. The Principle of Prior Consecration
   II. The Principle of Proper Motivation
 III. The Principle of Personal Responsibility

E ach of us must consider three important principles regarding how we use our money for the Lord. These aren't principles that sprang from my own mind; they came straight out of the Word of God. They are given to us in order to guide our giving and stewardship.

The Principle of Prior Consecration

Giving our resources to God is simply a reflection of the fact that we have already given ourselves to Him. We have dedicated our lives to the Lord, consecrating ourselves to His purposes, so it is only natural that we would also offer Him our financial resources. In 2 Corinthians 8:5, Paul said of the Macedonians, "They first gave themselves to the Lord, and then to us by the will of God." In other words, Paul knew that the believers in Macedonia had not only given an offering of money, but had given themselves to God. The highest, most noble calling for any Christian is that of commitment to Christ. When we do that, consecrating ourselves wholly to Him, financial stewardship is a natural outgrowth. Sacrificial giving is a reflex response to the One who loves us, for He gave His own Son on our behalf.

The principle of prior consecration recognizes the ownership by God of everything. He sovereignly controls all things. Every person in the world belongs to Him. As Paul puts it in Romans 14:8, "We are the Lord's." The prophet Ezekiel in 18:4 quotes God as saying, "All souls are Mine." And 1 Corinthians 6:20 tells us that we are not our own; we have been "bought at a price." The Lord owns us. He created us and paid for our souls with His own body. The principle of prior consecration simply recognizes that which is already true: We do not belong to ourselves, but to God. Everything we have is His. When we give an offering, it reflects the fact that we've already given ourselves to Him.

To offer God a gift without offering Him ourselves is shallow spirituality. In fact, we are reminded twice in the New Testament that if we are in church, ready to give a gift, and we realize there is something wrong in our hearts, we are to go and make it right before offering the gift. For you see, God is not anxious to collect our money. He is anxious to make us holy. Sometimes when I see some manipulative request for money on television, I ache for

God, because stewardship is to be a spiritual act. Giving an offering is a high and holy calling, a reflection of our spiritual state, rather than a bargain made with the Almighty. To give a gift without giving one's self is to violate the spiritual nature of New Testament giving. God is more interested in the giver than the gift. He wants us to be faithful in stewardship, not because He needs the money, but because it reveals our heart. What we do with our money is a barometer of our spirituality—a tangible method for revealing what we really believe.

If a man tells me he doesn't know what he believes, I have an answer for him: "Go home and read your checkbook." That will show him what is most important in his life. It is not possible to have the blessing of God if we keep our resources from Him. A man who withholds his finances from the Lord is not right with God. I've watched people come to Christ in worship services where I preached about stewardship, and I have found there is a direct relationship between what a man does spiritually and what he does financially. There are only two times most people walk the aisles of a church on Sunday: to commit to Christ and to collect the offering, and they are not unrelated! What we do with our money reveals what is important in our lives.

The Principle of Proper Motivation

I once had a man in my office say to me, "Pastor, those people in the Old Testament didn't have any choice. They had to give to God. They were under the Law and were dragged kicking and screaming into the Temple, bringing their offerings with them." My reply: "Do you think God honored those people?" There were undoubtedly some people who didn't want to give God an offering in Old Testament times, just as there are people who resent giving an offering today. But one thing I've learned from my studies in the Scriptures is that God is interested in our reasons for giving. He is just as interested in the motivations of a modern person as He was in the motivations of an Old Testament person.

In 2 Corinthians 9:7 we read, "So let each one give as he purposes in his heart, not grudgingly or of necessity; for God loves a cheerful giver." God doesn't want us to come to the offering loaded down with guilt. He doesn't want us to come reluctantly, grudgingly, or out of a sense of obligation. He wants our giving to be the spontaneous response of a loving heart toward God—giving cheerfully and willingly out of gratitude and love for Him.

As I studied the Old Testament, I found the same attitude present in every passage on giving. In Exodus 25:2 we find these words: "Speak to the children of Israel, that they bring Me an offering. From everyone who gives it willingly with his heart you shall take My offering." You see, God was interested in their motivation, not just their money. Similarly, in 1 Chronicles 29:9 we read, "Then the people rejoiced, for they had offered willingly, because with a loyal heart they had offered willingly to the LORD." These people were excited about being part of God's work, and they gave out of joy and gratitude. In the same way, Paul says this in Philippians 4:10: "I rejoiced in the Lord greatly that now at last your care for me has flourished again; though you surely did care, but you lacked opportunity." The believers were excited to be part of God's work through Paul, and the Lord appreciates that sort of motivation.

The Amplified Bible, which offers several synonyms for every important Greek and Hebrew word, translates 2 Corinthians 9:7 this way: "Let each one give as he has made up his own mind and purposed in his heart, not reluctantly or sorrowfully or under compulsion, for God loves (that is, He takes pleasure in, prizes above other things, and is unwilling to abandon or to do without) a cheerful (joyous, prompt-to-do-it) giver—whose heart is in his giving." So when we come to the offering, we ought to be excited, for we are given the opportunity to take part in God's great plan. As an expression of our love for Him, we give our gifts. After all He has done on our behalf, we can do no less.

A Christian doesn't give to the church, or to the budget, or even to the needs of the congregation. A Christian gives to the Lord, and it ought to excite him. If Jesus were to walk into a church service, most believers would give generously to Him, even taking off watches and rings or handing Him their car keys. They would be saying, "We love you, Lord, and we want to offer a tangible evidence of our love." But Jesus is in every service, so when the offering is taken we give with that same motivation and with an attitude of love and thanksgiving.

The Principle of Personal Responsibility

There is probably no deeper theological passage in all Scripture than 1 Corinthians 15. In that chapter Paul details the resurrection of Jesus Christ, which sets the Christian faith apart from every other religion. We have a Savior who came out of the grave, and our resurrection is the result of His resurrection. At the end of the chapter, Paul points out that because of this truth, we ought to be "steadfast, immovable, always abounding in the work of the Lord, knowing that your labor is not in vain in the Lord" (1 Corinthians 15:58). Then the Apostle immediately shifts his writing from the resurrection to the collection: "Now concerning the collection for the saints. . . . "

Paul understood the spiritual importance of giving, linking it to the believer's response to the triumph of Jesus Christ over the grave. "On the first day of the week let each one of you lay something aside, storing up as he may prosper, that there be no collections when I come," Paul states in 16:2. In that verse, he reveals who is responsible for supporting God's work: individual Christians. The church will not be held responsible for its giving, nor will Sunday School classes, families, or governments. The Bible teaches the principle of personal responsibility. Individuals will be asked to give an account of their use of finances at the end of time. "For we must all appear before the judgment seat of Christ, that each one may receive the things done in the body, according to what he has done, whether good or bad," it says in 2 Corinthians 5:10. To the Ephesians, Paul wrote, "Knowing that whatever good anyone does, he will receive the same from the Lord, whether he is a slave or free" (Ephesians 6:8). When we stand before God, we will be asked to account for everything. Whether rich or poor, young or old, each of us will have to give a personal accounting.

A church can have a huge budget, support many missionaries, give to local ministries, and even finance television and radio programs. But it can never go before God and claim, "Look what we are doing." God knows that the organization doesn't give— individuals do. He wants to know how the individuals are contributing, for each person holds responsibility to support the church.

Consider the personal pronouns used in these passages on stewardship:

"Concerning the collection . . . on the first day of the week let each one of you lay something aside . . . " (1 Corinthians 16:1, 2).

"He who sows sparingly will also reap sparingly" (2 Corinthians 9:6).

"So let each one give as he purposes in his heart . . . " (2 Corinthians 9:7).

Again, stewardship is a personal responsibility. The Bible's emphasis is always on the individual, not the church, the family, or the state. Every person will be asked to give an account, and he'll be allowed no sponsors or proxies to speak on his behalf. I believe in the priesthood of the believer. Each one of us stands or falls in the presence of God. I don't need a priest to take care of my soul. I am responsible for my own spiritual life. There is no hiding behind somebody else, and there will be no claiming that I didn't have to give because I belonged to a generous church. God doesn't care about my group activities as much as He cares about my personal responsibilities.

I don't pastor a church of wealthy individuals. There aren't a few millionaires who support everything we do. Instead, we have committed people who have made the decision to tithe because they understand their personal responsibility before God. Though some don't make much, they still understand that they're accountable for the small amount they do make. And they recognize that if they honor God, He will bless them. One young couple, who made the decision to start tithing, wrote me a letter and said, "We knew it was going to be hard, but we took the step. . . . And my husband has become more excited about spiritual things than ever before. Even our little boy came in the other day, so excited about Jesus he had been telling his friends about the Lord. There is a whole new spiritual tone to our family that we've never known before, and I can trace it right back to the point where we said, 'Okay, Lord, this is yours. We'll tithe in order to honor You.'"

God has promised to enable us to do what He has commanded. So get in line with His principles, give your life to Him, and start giving of your financial resources to Him.

1. What do the following passages have to say about the purpose of our giving?

   Proverbs 3:9 10

   2 Corinthians 8:13-15

   2 Corinthians 9:2, 12

   1 Timothy 5:17-18

   In your own words, how would you explain the principle of prior consecration?

   How is the principle illustrated in 2 Corinthians 8:5?

   What does 1 Peter 1:18-19 add to our understanding of the principle?

What does 2 Corinthians 9:7-8 say about our motivation for giving?

If someone asked you why you give so much money to the church, what would you say?

What has God done for you that motivates you to give to Him?

4. What clear teaching do you find in 1 Corinthians 16:2?

What do the words "as he may prosper" mean?

Why do you suppose Paul wanted the people to do this?

What principles for giving do you find in the following passages:

Proverbs 22:7

Matthew 22:21

Romans 13:8

Galatians 6:9-10

Philippians 4:19

1 Timothy 5:8

1 Timothy 6:6-10

Which of these principles could you apply in your own life?

Why is it important to remember that we are personally responsible for giving to God?

When do you find it easy to give?

When do you find it hard?

Aside from making more money, what would you like to change about your financial position? Why?

THE MEANING OF SACRIFICE

I n our self-centered world, it is sometimes hard to grasp the concept of *sacrifice*, and even harder to find examples of those who have made a sacrifice to God. This chapter will explore what sacrifice is and study the example of sacrifice made by our Lord.

   I. The Wealth That Was His
  II. The Poverty That Was His
 III. The Necessity of Sacrifice

I recently read an interview with a Hollywood movie star in which she was asked what gave her purpose for living. She replied that she lived for herself. Her greatest pleasure was found in pleasing herself, her only security was in herself, and her only sustaining love was with herself. She ended the interview by stating that the focus of her life was "the consummation of my own identity."

She is not alone in making that statement. Self-centeredness seems to be the philosophy of our day. We are surrounded by people who are committed only to themselves and their own happiness, openly flaunting the fact that the enhancement of their own personal pleasure is the driving force of their lives. Unfortunately, this philosophy has crept into the church and begun to influence the lives of God's people. The phrase "getting my needs met" seems to have replaced the Westminster Catechism in the language of modern saints. People leave churches because they can't find what they want.

Contrast that to the historic church. I stand amazed at the incongruity of singing words like, "All to Jesus I surrender, all to Him I freely give," or "Have thine own way, Lord," or even "Take my life and let it be, consecrated Lord to thee." Sometimes I wonder if our culture understands the biblical concept of sacrifice and the constant struggle it takes to achieve it. I choke on singing how "I surrender all" when in fact I'm holding back so much for myself!

We used to have a banner in our church sanctuary that read, "Not equal giving, but equal sacrifice." As I think about it, I question how many people understand the meaning of the word *sacrifice* anymore. It has a very different meaning today than it used to. The word originally came from two Latin words: *sacra*, which means "sacred," and *ficeo*, which means "to make." To sacrifice something was to make it sacred. The Jewish people understood its meaning, for at regular intervals they would select one perfect goat or lamb and bring it to the Temple in order to make it holy. They would give it to God, for it belonged to Him. God had entrusted all the flocks and herds to the people and demanded that occasionally they give some back to Him by sacrifice.

When Mary of Bethany anointed Jesus with an expensive jar of perfume, she sacrificed it, making it holy by giving it to God. When the poor widow of Luke 21 surrendered her two small coins for the Lord's work, she sacrificed them, making them holy unto God. In the early church, when the believers were sharing all things in common, occasionally someone would sell a house or land and give the money to the church, sacrificing it for God's purposes. In 2 Corinthians, we are told that the Macedonians not only gave out of their poverty, they begged for the opportunity to do so. They brought their gifts to the Apostle Paul and sacrificed them, making them holy unto God. The Bible is clear that there is nothing evil about having money. The Lord has entrusted some of it to us to be stewards of it for His sake. When we take some of that hard earned money and give it back to Him, we sacrifice it. It becomes a holy gift.

The Wealth That Was His

The one who illustrates this truth better than all others is Jesus Christ. In writing of Him, Paul once said that "though He was rich, yet for your sakes He became poor, that you through His poverty might become rich" (2 Corinthians 8:9). The Lord of Glory sacrificed riches and honor to become poor and humble. Imagine what it was like for Jesus to come to this world and give up the wealth that was His.

First, He sacrificed **a spiritual existence for a fleshly existence**. Modern philosophy teaches that flesh and blood is the highest form of being, but the Bible says that a spiritual being is greater than a fleshly being. Jesus existed in spirit, but He took upon Himself a body, becoming human and leaving the spiritual realm to take the form of a man. That was a step down—a sacrifice.

Second, He sacrificed **the presence of God for the presence of men**. The Bible tells us that Jesus was eternally present with the Father, but when He came to this earth He became Emmanuel, which means "God with us." He was no longer God with God, but God with us. Being with men can never compare to being with God. He took a step down—a sacrifice.

Third, He sacrificed **the beauty of heaven for the streets of earth**. The Scriptures teach us that heaven is a wonderful place, far more beautiful than anything here on earth. Jesus was willing to leave it, to sacrifice it, in order to walk the crowded streets of Jerusalem with men. He took a step down—a sacrifice. The Lord walked away from the wealth of heaven in order to come to man in poverty. He sacrificed all that was His to be here with us.

The Poverty That Was His

I'm not sure I know what it means for someone wealthy to make such a sacrifice as to become poor. But there are several things in Scripture that can help me to understand what Christ did when He gave up the wealth of heaven for the poverty of earth.

First, **He emptied Himself**. When Paul wrote to the Philippian church, he said that Jesus, "who, being in the form of God, did not consider it robbery to be equal with God, but made Himself of no reputation, taking the form of a bondservant, and coming in the likeness of men" (Philippians 2:6-7). That passage of Scripture which states that Christ "made Himself of no reputation" can also be translated, "He emptied Himself." That is, He gave up the richness of God's qualities in order to become a man. Had you walked the street of His village and seen the boy Jesus, you would not have recognized Him as God. He looked like any other young person. It wasn't until adulthood, when He began gathering His followers around Him, that it became apparent that Jesus was something other than an ordinary man. He left the right hand of the Father and came down here to walk the earth, surrounded by people who didn't even recognize His greatness.

Second, **He became a servant**. Jesus was not only poor in self-emptying, but poor in servanthood. Rather than come as an all-powerful sovereign, He came as a servant to all. One of the lasting impressions we have of Jesus is getting down on His knees to wash the dirty feet of His disciples. In poverty, He chose to become a servant.

Third, **He was poor in His sacrifice**. The Lord once noted that "Foxes have holes and birds of the air have nests, but the Son of Man has nowhere to lay His head" (Luke 9:58). Christ, who had been the occupant of heaven's glory, came to live in a place where He had no permanent home. He was born in a stable and wrapped in swaddling clothes, which were nothing more than rags—the clothing of poor people. So impoverished was He, the Lord of Glory didn't even have a place to lay His head. It is no wonder people struggled with the truth of Christ's deity. I can almost sense the awe of Paul as he writes, "Great is the mystery of godliness: God was manifested in the flesh" (1 Timothy 3:16).

The one who was rich in glory came to be poor on earth.

Yet the Bible says that Jesus became poor that we might be made rich. When He gave up the wealth of heaven to come to us, we became rich. It is because of His coming that we have the Spirit dwelling in our hearts and access to the throne of God. We can experience sweet fellowship, better than anything the world has to offer. We have been made rich through Christ's poverty.

The Necessity of Sacrifice

As I think about the history of the Christian church, I realize nothing great or godly ever happened that was not born out of sacrifice. Mothers recognize that fact, for the pain and travail of bringing a child into the world is great, but those children become even greater blessings. A mother must sacrifice herself, and go through a difficult time, to be able to experience the joy of a new life. No businessman I ever met would say that starting his business was easy. Pain and sacrifice preceded success. By sacrificing time and energy, a businessman eventually creates something worthwhile. Every Christian ministry in the country came into being because somebody, somewhere, was willing to sacrifice to start it.

We who live in a comfortable generation want good things to come without paying the price. We want the product without the process. We want the feast without the sacrifice. We want resurrection Sunday without Good Friday. But the Scriptures tell us things never work out that way. Whenever we want something worthwhile and eternal, we must always pay a price. Everything good requires sacrifice. Unless we're willing to pay the price, we can't experience those eternal things. Yet in the measure we are able to sacrifice, God can begin to do His work. As we make holy that which God has entrusted to us, He begins to use us as part of His mighty plan.

I once had the opportunity to visit a ministry to the homeless and the street people in San Diego. On a regular basis this man that God called ministers to forty people. He has purchased two dilapidated homes in the downtown area, in which his family lives with these poor souls. Some of them are coming off drugs, some have been sleeping in parks, and most haven't had a good meal in months. They have no place to go, no one to whom they can turn, so this minister takes them in. This man knows something about sacrifice. He has given everything to help those less fortunate than himself. Little by little, because of his sacrifice, others have come alongside to help him do the job. People who had no place to go now have a place to meet God, all because of one man's sacrifice.

As I studied the early history of the church I pastor, I found plenty of sacrifice. All the ministries were begun due to somebody's sacrifice of time, energy, and money. The schools were started because folks invested their time and sacrificed their money to start them. And today those ministries continue simply because people are willing to make a sacrifice and support them every month. And the funny thing is, those who make the sacrifices seem to be the happiest people I know. When asked, "Was it worth it?" they invariably reply, "I'd gladly do it all over again." To make a sacrifice is difficult, but it's the only way to accomplish great things.

In Charles Colson's wonderful book, *Loving God*, he shares a piece of history that beautifully illustrates the importance of sacrifice. A fourth-century Asiatic monk by the name of Telemachus spent most of his life in a remote community, praying and raising vegetables for the cloistered community. When he was not tending his garden, Telemachus fulfilled the vocation of studying prayer. One day the monk felt the Lord wanted him to go to Rome, the biggest and busiest city on earth. He had no idea why God wanted him there, and the thought of being in Rome terrified him, but as that monk prayed he clearly sensed the voice of God telling him to go. This bewildered monk set out on the long journey over dusty roads, everything he owned on his back, heading toward a city he didn't know. But he obediently followed the Lord's lead, arriving in the city during the holiday season.

At that time the Roman rulers kept the ghettos quiet by providing bread and entertainment, and Telemachus found himself in the midst of a jubilant commotion. He thought God had some special role for him to play, so he let the crowds guide him, and the stream of humanity soon led him to the coliseum, where the gladiator contests were staged. The monk could hear the cries of the caged animals and had a premonition of terrible violence, realizing the crowd had come to be amused at the sight of men killing one another. Telemachus could not sit still and watch such savagery, yet neither could he leave the crowd and forget the violence, so in frustration he jumped on top of the perimeter wall and shouted, "In the name of Christ, forbear!"

No one paid the slightest attention to him, and the fighting began, to the cheers of the crowd. So that little monk plodded down the stone steps onto the sandy floor of the arena, a scrawny man in a monk's habit dashing around among the armed athletes. One gladiator sent him sprawling with the thrust of a shield, but the monk again cried out, "In the name of Christ, forbear!" The crowd began to laugh at him, some cheering him on, thinking he was part of the entertainment. Then his movements blocked the vision of one contestant, annoyed at this man in his way. "Run him through!" someone shouted, and with a flash of steel, the gladiator struck Telemachus, slashing across his chest and stomach. As he drew his last breath, the little monk gasped out once more, "In the name of Christ, forbear."

Then a strange thing happened. As everyone focused on the still form of Telemachus lying on the crimson sand, the arena grew quiet. In the silence, someone near the top of the coliseum stood up and walked out. Someone else followed Soon the spectators were streaming out of that arena, until there was no one left to watch. The innocent figure lying in a pool of blood crystallized the opposition, and it was the last gladiatorial event ever held in a Roman coliseum. Never again did men kill each other for the crowd's entertainment. And it was all because one scrawny monk who believed in something was willing to sacrifice himself to make it happen.

Everything worthwhile is built on sacrifice. Creating strong homes and churches takes sacrifice, as believers stand up for moral purity in a world polluted with immorality. Supporting the work of the ministry requires sacrifice, as Christians forego some worldly pleasures in order to fund the work of God in the world. Nothing good ever came easy, and if we did not have those willing to sacrifice, the ministry of the church would disappear in the world.

Of course, most of us are not asked to give our lives as Telemachus did. Yet, in a world inundated with selfish celebrities and selfish messages, we must decide what we're willing to sacrifice. The purpose of this study on stewardship is to move us away from selfishly thinking about "our needs" and toward the example of that monk. In the process of doing that, we'll start to see our lives changed and God work in our midst. If we'll only learn to sacrifice, we can begin to see the power of God at work.

1. What do you think of when you hear the word *sacrifice*?

What does it mean?

In your opinion, do most people view making a sacrifice as
something positive or negative? Why?

Who do you know that has made the greatest sacrifices?

Why did he or she make them?

What sacrifices have you had to make in your life?

What did people sacrifice in Old Testament times, and why was that meaningful?

How is that similar to the sacrifices Christians are called upon to make today?

In what way is giving money to the church a sacrifice?

Who are some biblical characters that made a sacrifice of some kind for God?

Which character do you relate to? Why?

What do the following passages reveal about making sacrifices:

Psalm 51:17-19

Matthew 9:13

Romans 12:1-2

1 Corinthians 10:20

Philippians 4:14-19

Hebrews 13:15-16

1 Peter 2:4-5

6. In your own words, what did Jesus Christ sacrifice in coming to earth?

Why was He willing to make such sacrifices?

What feelings does that engender in your heart, to know that He made sacrifices for you?

What do you learn about Christ's sacrifice in the following verses:

Isaiah 53: 1-12

Ephesians 5:1-2

Hebrews 9:23-28

Hebrews 10:5-13

DID YOU KNOW

In Old Testament times, the High Priest was continually making sacrifices on behalf of the people. As a matter of fact, there were no chairs in the Temple, for the sins of the people necessitated a constant sacrifice before God. Yet Hebrews 10:12 offers a remarkable lesson about the sacrifice of Jesus Christ, noting that "this Man, after He had offered one sacrifice for sins forever, sat down at the right hand of God." Christ's death on the cross was the last sacrifice for sin we would ever need!

THREE-DIMENSIONAL GIVING

A few days before His death, Jesus sat in a friend's home and received a wonderful gift of love. The person who made that gift, and the response of another to her extravagance, reveal to us some important principles for healthy stewardship.

I. Mary: The Positive Principles of a Giving Heart
II. Judas: The Negative Principles of a Selfish Heart

One of the best lessons I ever learned in Bible study methods was the lesson of "truth in tension." The Bible is careful to present both sides of an issue, so we can see it in balance. That is never more perfectly illustrated than in character studies. God delights in showing us the life of one person against the backdrop of someone else. For instance, the Lord teaches us about the generous character of Abraham by contrasting it with the selfishness of Lot. The contrast allows us to appreciate the influence of each life, and the results of the choices we make.

In John 12, there is a wonderful contrast made between Mary and Judas, and unless you see each person's motives clearly, you cannot appreciate their character. To really explore this passage, it is important to remember when this event occurred in the life of Christ. He had just raised Lazarus from the dead, exciting the crowds but earning the enmity of the Jewish leaders. As a matter of fact, John 11:53 tells us that those leaders were so upset over the Lord's display of power they began plotting to kill Jesus.

So Christ left the area, going to a desert city called Ephraim before leaving to celebrate Passover in Jerusalem. The other gospel accounts tell us that along the way, Jesus called Zacchaeus to repentance, healed blind Bartimaeus, and visited His friend Lazarus whom He had raised from the dead. Finally the Lord came to rest at the home of Mary, Martha, and Lazarus, in the city of Bethany, just outside Jerusalem. It is here that John's gospel gives us a clear account of an amazing event in the life of Christ. The story was given to us for a purpose, so that we can contrast the actions and attitudes of Mary with those of Judas Iscariot and understand the results of their different choices.

Mary: The Positive Principles of a Giving Heart

As you read John 12:1-11, you find that Mary demonstrates for us the **sacrificial attitude** essential to Christian giving. The text says that she "took a pound of very costly oil of spikenard" (v. 3). The expensive nature of this oil can best be understood by examining the attention Judas gave it. That man, who knew about money and was put in charge of the disciples' purse, sized up the value of that gift in verse 5: "Why was this fragrant oil not sold for three hundred denarii and given to the poor?" Now at that time, a denarii was equal to about one day's pay, so Mary's gift of oil was awfully extravagant—equal to nearly one year's wages! It was an incredible sacrifice in a time when most people earned their living one day at a time.

As a pastor, there have been times when we have asked people to give a day's wages to a special project. I've even known ministries that have asked people to offer a week's wages to something important. But I have never heard of a church or ministry asking someone to sacrifice one year's wages for any project. Yet that's exactly what Mary did. She offered to the Lord Jesus something extremely valuable.

Keep in mind that Mary had recently buried her own brother. Lazarus was then resurrected, but that still meant Mary had gone through the burial rituals. I find it interesting that she had not used the expensive oil for her brother's funeral, but when the time came gave it to Jesus in a lavish show of love and affection. Her actions support something King David once claimed: that he would not give God that which had cost him nothing. We don't give God our leftovers; they are worth nothing to Him. Instead, we give Him that which costs us something. Mary's actions reveal the principle of a sacrificial attitude.

Second, Mary demonstrates the **servant attitude** of giving. Luke 12:3 reads, "Mary . . . anointed the feet of Jesus, and wiped His feet with her hair. And the house was filled with the fragrance of the oil." Others had come to the Lord and waited to receive something from Him, but Mary came to give the Lord His due. She knelt and worshipped Him, and Christ commended her for it. When we give, it ought to be with that same spirit. We give willingly, lovingly, not because we want to receive something, but because we want to serve our Lord.

A pastor once told me that every time his phone rings, somebody wants something. Perhaps that's as it should be, for pastors are servants to the body of Christ. But once in a while I'll get a phone call where somebody says, "Pastor, I was just praying for you, and I wanted to call and tell you I love you. I don't want anything. I just want to let you know how much we appreciate you." Those are always exciting, encouraging calls for a pastor. And that's just what Mary did for Jesus. She came in a submissive manner, not wanting anything other than to pour out her love for Him. God delights in that sort of servant's attitude.

Third, Mary demonstrates for us the **submissive attitude** of giving. She lavished an expensive gift upon the Savior, pouring it on His feet. Her humility was demonstrated in the fact that she let down her hair in public, a rare event in Jewish culture, showing that she was without concern for the acceptance of others. Mary didn't care what anyone else thought. She just wanted the Lord to know of her great love. She gave her best, gave it lovingly and lavishly, in spite of any criticism.

Fourth, Mary reveals to us the **scriptural attitude** essential for Christian giving. The joy of giving comes from sincerely showing our love for God. Mary gave her gift to Jesus because she believed He was God. She understood that something important was about to happen, something not even the disciples believed yet, that the Lord was about to die. "She has kept this for the day of My burial," Jesus says in verse 7, and Mary's action was part of the preparation process. This was the only anointing Jesus' body received, for His death and burial were hurried so as not to interfere with Jewish holidays. We must assume that God somehow put into Mary's mind the darkness of the hour. She was determined that Jesus, who was about to die on behalf of His people, deserved to be anointed, and she wanted to get it done while the opportunity was there. She accepted the fact that there would be no time for the usual niceties, though the rest of His followers failed to see the importance of the events.

Fifth, Mary demonstrates the **serious attitude** which is necessary in giving. Her gift to the Lord was serious business, so when given the opportunity, she gave. Had Mary waited, she would have missed the chance. Jesus understood that same fact, for He said, "The poor you have with you always, but Me you do not have always" (v. 8). He would only go to the cross once, and this was the one chance His followers had to anoint Him for burial. Remember, other women came to anoint Him after His death, but His body was already wrapped up and placed into a tomb. They gathered their love gifts, but it was already too late.

That reminds me of some Christians who are always waiting for a more convenient time to give to God. When they are young, they don't have enough money, so they wait to give. When they have families, they wait until the children are grown. When the children are grown, they wait until all their education is paid off. When that's done, they're too busy socking away money for retirement. Their lives have passed by while they've waited for an opportunity to give. But you see, we can never afford to give—that's why giving is such a sacrifice! My wife and I couldn't afford to get married, but we did anyway because we were in love. When I came to grips with the fact that I had to commit my whole life to the Lord, I stopped worrying about when I could afford to give. I just started giving, and God took care of the rest. One day each of us will stand before the Lord to give an account, and if we have wasted all our opportunities we'll have nothing to say. The opportunities are there; we just have to make use of them.

Finally, Mary demonstrates the **spiritual attitude** which we all need to have in giving. She saw the great spiritual nature of giving. Her eye was on the future. She gave her today for God's tomorrow. She invested in the Lord, and her action created a memorial that is forever remembered. As Matthew puts it in his gospel, "Assuredly, I say to you, wherever this gospel is preached in the whole world, what this woman has done will also be told as a memorial to her" (Matthew 26:13). Monuments to great men have come and gone, nations have risen and fallen, but Mary's gift of oil endures. No one reads the story of Jesus without hearing of Mary's gracious act of giving. Giving is a spiritual action, not merely a physical one, and Mary demonstrated an understanding of that.

Judas: The Negative Principles of a Selfish Heart

A reading of John 12 would not be complete unless we contrast the positive attitude of Mary with the negative attitude of Judas. He illustrates all that can go wrong with stewardship and giving. Just as Mary is the example of what we ought to be, Judas is the example of what we ought not to be. Notice how the Bible characterizes him so carefully, demonstrating a deceitful attitude which needs to be avoided by Christians. In verses 4-6 we read, "One of His disciples, Judas Iscariot, Simon's son, who would betray Him, said, 'Why was this fragrant oil not sold for three hundred denarii and given to the poor?' This he said, not that he cared for the poor, but because he was a thief, and had the money box; and he used to take what was put in it."

Just as Mary's selfless giving became a monument to her love, Judas' selfish concern became a monument to his own evil character. No one names their son Judas any more, for the very name has come to mean betrayal and wickedness. This false disciple offered nothing but a pious excuse. Judas didn't care for the poor. He simply wanted the appearance of having great spiritual concern in order to cover up his own greed. He was trying to make people believe he was something he was not. In doing so, Judas demonstrates a **deceitful attitude**.

One thing I've learned as a pastor is that some people will try to deceive others by appearing pious. After a building dedication, I had someone tell me that a man had been shaking his head, muttering that we had wasted our money. "What we're doing is a shame," he told people. "There are so many needy people in this city. We ought to be giving our money to them instead of building this big place." But when I asked who it was that had spoken, I wasn't at all surprised to discover that it was a man who had never given a thing to God. He was deceitful and dishonest, but extremely pious about the Lord's work. Like Judas, he wanted to appear spiritual without having to make any actual sacrifices.

In addition, Judas demonstrated a **dishonest attitude**. He didn't really want to give money to the poor. He wanted to get that money into the money bag so he could use some of it for himself. Judas saw a wonderful opportunity to replenish his personal resources go down the drain, so he resented Mary's extravagant gift. No doubt Judas would have worked out a scheme for embezzling the money. It was no accident that his last act was selling the Lord of heaven for thirty pieces of silver. The kiss he planted on Christ's cheek in the Garden of Gethsemane wasn't a moment of weakness, but the culmination of a lifelong hunger for money. Judas was a thief, taking what belonged to God and spending it on himself.

We don't give to God out of guilt, for that doesn't honor Him. At the same time, we had better decide if we're going to believe the Bible and obey its call to give, for failure to give our offerings to God also doesn't honor Him. Our choice is to be a Mary and give generously to the Lord, or to be a Judas and fail to give Him anything. Either way, we help to create our own monument. I'm convinced that if Christians will explore what the Bible has to say about giving, and begin to obey God's commands, the needs of the church will be met. There is no concern about raising enough money; the concern is about raising up obedient believers. Giving is a spiritual concern, and each of us will decide if we're going to be obedient or disobedient to God's call. The choice we make will have eternal results.

1. What is the most extravagant gift someone has given you?

    What is the most extravagant gift you have ever given someone?

    What was your motivation in giving such a lavish gift?

    Read John 12:1-8. Who was Mary?

    What had recently happened in her family?

Why were these days before the Passover so important to Jesus?

What was special about Mary's action toward Jesus?

How do you suppose the rest of Christ's followers responded to her actions?

In your own words, how would you describe Mary's motivation for her actions?

What was Judas' response?

Why did he respond that way?

How can someone's financial choices become a monument to his life?

What do the following passages of Scripture reveal about the faithfulness of God:

Psalm 18:2

Psalm 36:5

Psalm 89:1-8

Psalm 92:1-2

Psalm 100:5

Psalm 143:1

Isaiah 40:8

Lamentations 3:23

1 Corinthians 10:13

2 Corinthians 1:18-20

1 Thessalonians 5:23-24

2 Thessalonians 3:3

1 John 1:9

What does the fact that God is faithful inspire in you?

What do the following verses require of our own faithfulness to God:

1 Corinthians 4:2

1 Timothy 3:11

2 Timothy 2:2

What does our faithfulness to God result in, according to Proverbs 28:20?

In slaughter houses today, a goat is selected and trained to help the men in their work. The job of that special goat is to lead the sheep from the pens into the slaughter house. As a memorial to one man, that goat is called "the Judas goat."

GOD'S
HARVEST
LAW

The Scriptures say that a man reaps what he sows. It is God's law of the harvest. Not only is it true in planting seeds, but also in the investment of our time and treasures. This chapter will explore the ramifications of God's harvest law.

 I. The Principles of God's Harvest Law
 II. The Products of God's Harvest Law
III. The Perfect Example of God's Harvest Law

R.G. LeTourneau, a manufacturer of earth-moving equipment, loved the Lord Jesus Christ. He had started his business during the Depression and made $35,000 his first year. Puffed up with pride, LeTourneau decided to withhold his annual commitment to his church in order to reinvest his money into his business. He believed that if he could make a big return on his investment, the Lord's work would have an even greater amount the next year. But God is not mocked. By withholding the tithe from the storehouse, LeTourneau was playing games with God. Rather than making money, the next year he lost $100,000! Chastened, R.G. LeTourneau got down on his knees and repented before God. He committed himself to faithfully returning what he had taken, regardless of the company deficit. His fortune changed that very moment, and from that time on his entire life was different. Within four years, he had created the LeTourneau Foundation, comprised of 90% of the stock in his company, which has financed evangelical works all over the globe ever since.

LeTourneau liked to talk about the two loves of his life: turning on the machines he designed and watching them work, and turning on the power of the Gospel and watching it work. He did well in both of those areas. R.G. LeTourneau held over 200 patents, and the equipment he designed is in use all over the world, so he was certainly able to watch his machines work. But he also gave 90% of his income to Christian ministry and presented the Gospel to people throughout the world, so he had the opportunity to watch the Gospel work.

Shortly before he died, LeTourneau wrote of having learned the "great harvest law" of the New Testament. That law is simple: we reap what we sow. If a man sows little, he will reap little. If he sows much, he will reap much. LeTourneau enjoyed explaining to people the principle that we must give money back to God if we expect to succeed financially. "It is not how much money I give to God that is important," LeTourneau liked to say. "It is how much of God's money I keep for myself that's important."

In 2 Corinthians 9, the Apostle Paul details the harvest law of God and explains why our relationship with the Lord is tied to our offerings for the Lord. There are three basic things we need to examine about ourselves and our walk with God.

The Principles of God's Harvest Law

God's Word offers us several principles for helping us experience His harvest. First is the **principle of investment**. Paul says in 2 Corinthians 9:6, "But this I say: He who sows sparingly will also reap sparingly, and he who sows bountifully will also reap bountifully." Simply put, if you don't sow, you won't reap. Consider this: In one kernel of corn is all the potential of a reproducing cycle. If I plant the kernel, it will reproduce itself and bring forth many times the original kernel. Each of those new kernels can be planted, so that I now have thousands of kernels. That cycle goes on and on. But if I take that kernel of corn and, enamored with its potential, put it in a frame over my fireplace so it can be admired, it will be of no value. The only way that kernel can be valuable to me is if it is invested and used.

Many Christians today need to learn the principle of investment. As long as we hold onto the things God has given us, refusing to sow them back into the harvest field, we will never have any more. The reason so few wealthy people have found lasting happiness is because they haven't learned the importance of the principle of investment. In the words of Andrew Carnegie, "Millionaires who laugh are rare."

I recently read the story of a wealthy man who, in old age, became obsessed with the idea that something was wrong with his hands. When his wife sent for a doctor, he found the man staring at his hands in horror. "Look at them," he said, "They're so empty, so very empty. I've spent my life amassing what I could hold, and now there is nothing to show for it." A man reaps what he sows. One cannot have the blessing of God if he is unwilling to take the resources entrusted to him and invest them back into the harvest field. Money must be invested if it is to create something of value. That's the principle of investment.

Second is the **principle of identity**. Not only do we get if we sow, but we get what we sow. That is, if I plant corn, I'll get more corn. I cannot plant corn and expect carrots. Whatever I plant is what I'll get. Paul once wrote, "He who sows to his flesh will of the flesh reap corruption, but he who sows to the Spirit will of the Spirit reap everlasting life" (Galatians 6:8). A man reaps exactly what he sows. If he sows anger and discord, his life will be filled with trouble. If he sows callousness, he will find his life filled with unloving relationships.

I like being around joyful people because I find that when they are with me, they sow joy in my life. When I'm around positive people, my outlook just seems to be brighter. Perhaps one of the reasons there is so much ingratitude in the world is because we haven't expressed thankfulness and appreciation enough. But there are no surprises—we'll get what we sow. Therefore we ought to consider sowing the things of the Lord.

Third is the **principle of increase**. God has arranged for things to grow and develop. If a farmer planted a kernel of corn, waited for six months, and only got one more kernel of corn, there would be no sense in reproducing it. There is no future if there is no increase. But the Bible is clear that sowing leads to increase. If we sow bountifully, we shall reap bountifully. If the first principle says "I get if I sow," and the second principle says "I get what I sow," then this third principle says "I get more than I sow."

"Now may He who supplies seed to the sower, and bread for food, supply and multiply the seed you have sown and increase the fruits of your righteousness," Paul writes in 2 Corinthians 9:10. When we sow, we get an abundance in return. In explaining this concept to the Corinthian church, Paul actually uses the Greek word for "abundance" in verses 6, 8, 11, and 12. He wanted them to recognize the fact that when we invest with God, He knows how to return abundantly. Whatever we give to Him will increase. "God is able to make all grace abound toward you, that you, always having all sufficiency in all things, may have an abundance for every good work" (v. 8).

Fourth is the **principle of interval**. We will reap what we sow, but it takes a while. We reap long after we sow. The farmer goes to his field, plants his corn, and waits. He doesn't come back that afternoon to reap, and he doesn't quit if he hasn't seen any cornstalks sprouting by the next day. One of the lessons of the harvest is that good things take time. Yet I've watched Christians make great promises to God regarding giving, then get discouraged the very next week when their financial problems didn't disappear.

Nobody expects to sow and reap on the same day. Paul said in Galatians 6:9, "Let us not grow weary while doing good, for in due season we shall reap if we do not lose heart." My parents poured their lives into a church and school in Dayton, Ohio, for 25 years. They invested their time, talents, and treasures into seeing that work grow, but they never benefited financially. Yet if you asked them if it was worth it, they would tell you the harvest is just coming in. The young people they trained are starting to impact the world for the cause of Jesus Christ. It's been a long interval, but all that cultivating and watering is starting to pay off. Remember the promise of Hebrews 6:10: "For God is not unjust to forget your work and labor of love which you have shown toward His name, in that you have ministered to the saints, and do minister." You may think He has forgotten your sacrifice, but the Lord remembers. His ability to keep the laws of the harvest operating is not in question. So take a look at the results of that investment in our lives.

The Products of God's Harvest Law

When we follow the principles of God's harvest law, we eventually begin to see what they produce. First, **we begin to prosper spiritually and financially**. Take another look at 2 Corinthians 9:10: "Now may He who supplies seed to the sower, and bread for food, supply and multiply the seed you have sown." As we give to the Lord, He in turn multiplies what we have. And God is able to make sure we always have enough.

Second, as we follow His principles, **we prove our love for God**. Our giving demonstrates our devotion to Him. "While, through the proof of this ministry, they glorify God for the obedience of your confession to the gospel of Christ, and for your liberal sharing with them and all men" (v. 13). An offering to the Lord is a tangible evidence of the reality of our commitment. It's easy to claim to love Him, but when we give sacrificially to Him we prove our love. Actually, it's difficult for me to comprehend how a man can love God, yet never use his money to do anything for God's kingdom. I don't think God believes him, and I'm not sure the man really believes it himself.

Third, when we obey the command to give, **we provide for those in need**. "The administration of this service not only supplies the needs of the saints, but also is abounding through many thanksgivings to God" (v. 12). Like many churches, we keep a fund to support those in times of financial hardship. Yet people are not merely in need of physical help—they also need spiritual help. Thus we provide a pastoral staff to help people grow in their walk with God, a facility where they can meet, and the utilities so they'll have lights and water. The reason we take a collection each Sunday is not to pay the light bill but to enable the Lord's work to continue and to provide for the needs of His people.

Fourth, one of the products of giving to God is that **we provoke many thanksgivings to the Lord**. Whenever someone gives, he starts a chain reaction of thanksgivings. In 2 Corinthians 9 there are three references to this: verse 11 tells us it creates thanksgiving, verse 12 echoes that thought, and verse 15 simply cries out, "Thanks be to God for His indescribable gift!"

As we put our money into the offering plate, it goes into a church treasury. Then a check is sent off to a mission board, which allows God's missionaries to go out and spread the Good News. The mission agency translates the dollars into the coinage of the country in which they serve, and one day an envelope arrives with a support check that says, "We love you and we're glad to be sponsoring you in the field." The people at the church thank God that they've been able to keep the church's commitment. The people at the mission agency thank God that He has been faithful in taking care of their people. The missionaries thank God that so many Christians are supporting them in their work. The souls to whom they introduce the saving knowledge of Jesus Christ lift their voices in praise of God's mercy in allowing them to meet these missionaries and know the truth. And, eventually, the members of that church hear about all the good things happening in the mission field and they give thanks to God for allowing them to be part of His mighty plan on earth. When we give, we create a cascade of thanksgivings to His name.

Fifth, when we give **we promote prayer**. As soon as that missionary opens his letter, he drops his head and begins praying to the Lord. He doesn't just say thanks, but he remembers to pray for the work of that sponsoring church and his many friends who have supported him through the years. And everyone else involved in the process also starts praying, so that the dynamic of God's great harvest law just keeps growing. Only eternity will reveal to us the far-reaching impact we have when we give to His work from the abundance He has entrusted to us.

Sixth, as we involve ourselves in giving, **we purchase greater opportunity to give again**. I don't know all the reasons why God blesses those who give, but I know at least one: He blesses them so they can give again! "God is able to make all grace abound toward you, that you, always having all sufficiency in all things, have an abundance for every good work" (v. 8). Remember, the farmer sets aside some of his harvest so he can plant again next year. Then the process continues time after time. Similarly, we just keep giving to God, knowing that as we sow, we shall reap.

The Perfect Example of God's Harvest Law

One last element remains to be considered in this text: the excitement and joy which ought to come with giving. When the Apostle Paul finished this great passage on giving, he was so filled with joy he had to exclaim, "Thanks be to God!" That's exactly what happens to us when we give.

Yet there is a sobering thought to God's harvest laws: If He was to reap many sons to glory, He would have to sow His own Son. Therefore the Father summoned the best heaven had to offer in the person of the Lord Jesus Christ, sent Him to earth, and allowed Him to die so others could live. Like that kernel of corn, the death of Jesus Christ allows the resurrection of many sons and daughters of God. Because He was sown, we have been reaped. Jesus is the perfect example of God's harvest laws.

If God, in His wisdom and love, believed in the importance of the harvest enough to send His own Son, we too must follow His example. We must believe in the sowing of seed so that we can reap a great harvest. We must be willing to give to God, that He might begin to use us in His plan for the ages, harvesting souls for the kingdom.

1. Read 2 Corinthians 8:1-15. What do you learn about the
    Macedonian churches?

    Were they wealthy or poor?

    What was their attitude in giving?

    Why did they give money to support Paul's work?

    What was the result of their giving?

2. What encouragement does Paul offer in verse 7?

According to verse 8, what did he want to test?

What example did Jesus set for us in giving, according to verse 9?

3. What is the meaning of verse 11?

How would you reword verse 12 for a modern person?

What was Paul's main point, according to verses 13-15?

4. What is the principle of investment?

In what are you investing?

5. What is the principle of identity?

How is that related to giving?

6. How would you define the principle of increase?

When have you experienced this principle at work in your life?

7. What is the principle of interval?

How would you respond to someone who complained, "I started tithing recently, and now I'm in worse financial shape than ever!"

8. Why do you suppose we prosper spiritually when we give?

When have you enjoyed giving something away?

Describe how your tithing provokes thanksgiving and promotes prayer.

The nation of Macedonia was a Roman province when Paul wrote his letter to the church at Corinth. It is most famous for having conquered much of the world under the brilliant military leader Alexander the Great, but his empire quickly fell apart after his untimely death. Today that area consists of parts of Greece and the nations of Albania and Macedonia. Paul established flourishing churches in the Macedonian cities of Philippi, Thessalonica, and Berea, and he often spoke warmly of the believers in those churches.

WHEN WE FORGET GOD

HAGGAI   1 : 1 - 11

W hen God commanded Israel to rebuild the temple, He expected His people to obey. At first there was great enthusiasm, but as the initial joy wore off, people started thinking more about themselves than the Lord. This chapter will explore the message of the prophet Haggai, who called the people to complete their commitment to God.

   I.   The Excuse
  II.   The Exhortation
 III.   The Encouragement

W here did all the money go?" Have you ever found yourself saying those words? Have you ever looked at your
checkbook at the end of a pay period, or the month, or
the year, and wondered? How easily expenditures fall outside the
boundaries of our earnings, and how easily inflation attacks our
savings!

Five hundred years before the birth of Jesus Christ, another
culture experienced that same struggle. They faced an inflation
that would stagger the imagination of modern economists. The
people earned reasonable wages, but before they could turn
around, it was all spent. The prophet Haggai says it was as though
the people had holes in their pockets, for money seemed to go
right through their hands, and they had nothing to show for it.
The Jews who were trying to resettle Jerusalem just couldn't seem
to keep ahead of their money, and the prophet used their
economic situation as the basis for reminding them of their
responsibilities. "You looked for much, but indeed it came to little;
and when you brought it home, I blew it away," the Lord says in
Haggai 1:9. Why did God make sure the people had no money?
Because "My house . . . is in ruins, while every one of you runs to
his own house." In other words, the people were taking care of
their own homes, but they were neglecting the house of God.

In order to better understand the prophet's message, let's go
back a little bit and examine the history of Haggai's time. For 70
long years, the nation of Israel was in captivity to Babylon. At the
end of that time, a Persian king by the name of Cyrus gave permis-
sion to a group of Jews to leave Babylon and return to Jerusalem
in order to restore the city which a previous king had flattened.
According to Ezra 2:64, there were 42,360 Jews who left Babylon
and returned to Jerusalem. Their first task was to restore the
Temple, which had lain in waste all those years. In Old Testament
culture the Temple was a sacred place. The glory of God actually
resided in the Temple. Without it, there was no central place of
worship for the Jews.

Like any big building project, it was a huge task. At first there
was remarkable enthusiasm as the people cleared the rubbish,
cleaned the site, and built a foundation for the altar. The Scripture
says that before any actual building began, the people took the

altar of God and restored it to its central place. There were no walls and no foundations for the outer walls, but the altar was in place. At that point, Ezra tells us that the crowds got so excited they began to sing and dance and praise God. Their central place of worship was restored. But soon their enthusiasm began to wane. They stopped the building of the Temple. Some opposition arose, and some people tried to press the local leadership to prohibit any more construction, so the Jews grabbed onto this excuse to stop building.

Perhaps you have experienced something like that in your spiritual life. Many people, when they first meet Christ, are excited and happy. But as time goes along, they lose that initial fervor. The Bible records that once the altar of the Temple was placed, the building stopped. But God sent His prophet, Haggai, to stir the people up and get them moving in the right direction. You might think you've heard burning sermons in your life, but you've probably never heard anything like Haggai's preaching! He said everything that needed to be said. He confronted the people for refusing to do what God would have them do. As we examine his sermon, we find there are three parts to it: the excuse, the exhortation, and the encouragement.

The Excuse

"Thus speaks the LORD of hosts, saying, 'This people says, "The time has not come, the time that the Lord's house should be built"'" (Haggai 1:2). That was the excuse the people of Israel used: They had decided it wasn't time to rebuild the Temple. It wasn't that it was a bad idea, and they would get to it some day, but the timing was wrong. They wanted to wait for a better day. That is a common excuse among those who don't want to give.

It was harvest time, according to Haggai, and times were hard for these people. They all wanted to go back to their fields and harvest their crops. They didn't have time to do what God wanted them to do, so they reasoned the time wasn't right. How many projects has God directed us to complete, and we have postponed them because it didn't seem the time was right? We're always looking for a convenient way out of obeying God, and one of the easiest excuses is procrastination. "Not now. I'll get to it later." I've known many people who use that excuse when it comes to tithing. They mean to do it, and one of these days they plan to start, but now isn't the right time. They first have to pay some bills, or get some things in order, so they wait until they're in a better financial position, and all they're really doing is saying no to God. They know it's the right thing to do, but they don't do it. Then they make themselves feel better by promising to do it "later." That's an excuse, and it was the same excuse Israel used to keep from accomplishing God's work.

The Exhortation

"Then the word of the LORD came by Haggai the prophet, saying, 'Is it time for you yourselves to dwell in your paneled houses, and this temple to lie in ruins?'" (vv. 3-4). The prophet noticed something about the people. They had time to build their own houses, but not the house of God. In fact, they didn't just build plain houses; they built themselves some pretty fancy homes for the time. The phrase "paneled houses" refers to a nice home made with wooden beams inside. It was an uncommon thing, for in Judah timber was not plentiful, so quite possibly the people were taking the timber they gathered and, rather than using it to build the Temple, they were redirecting it to build their own homes.

Haggai saw the Temple of God lying in waste, noticed the nice homes people were living in, and pointed out the incongruity. They had forgotten the importance of the project, forgotten how the Lord had allowed them to come back to their country, and forgotten the task to which He had called them. Once in the land, the people had gotten caught up in their own net worth and started diverting resources to themselves that actually belonged to God.

The actions of the people reveal the attitude of their hearts. Their worship was confined to a bare minimum: an altar in a bare field. They would come from their nice houses, worship around that altar, and tell themselves everything was all right. So Haggai reminded them not only of their forgetful attitude, but of the futility of their accumulation of goods. "Now therefore, thus says the LORD of hosts: 'Consider your ways! You have sown much, and bring in little; you eat, but do not have enough; you drink, but you are not filled with drink; you clothe yourselves, but no one is warm; and he who earns wages, earns wages to put into a bag with holes'" (vv. 5-6).

The people had an insatiable desire for more. They had turned their attention from God to the accumulation of goods, and the prophet was warning them to think about what they were doing. What happens to a man when he starts acting that way? He grabs more and more stuff, but it's never enough. He can't get enough toys, can't get enough food and drink, can't wear enough nice clothes. It's like sticking his money into a bag with holes where it just keeps falling out.

Then Haggai says, "'You looked for much, but indeed it came to little; and when you brought it home, I blew it away. Why?' says the LORD of hosts. 'Because of My house that is in ruins, while every one of you runs to his own house'" (v. 9). The people thought they were getting ahead by neglecting God's priorities, but in reality they were accomplishing nothing. God's plans were not being achieved, and the plans of the people were not being accomplished. While all their energies, resources, and money were being directed upon themselves, their actual net worth wasn't increasing. Inflation and spending was eating up everything they hoped to gain.

One of the things I have noticed with my own finances is that if I trust God, things that look impossible become possible. One of the great surprises is that regular, systematic stewardship to the Lord somehow stretches our resources so they meet all our needs. On the other hand, when we try to hold out on God in order to build our own net worth, we never seem to get ahead. As one old preacher put it, "When God gets His, and I get mine, then everything is just fine. But if I get mine and take God's too, what do you think God will do? I think He'll collect, don't you?"

Haggai said to the people, "If you think you can take what belongs to God and redirect it to yourselves, you're fooling yourselves. It will slip through your fingers. You're going to end up no further along than you would have been if you'd given to God in the first place." The accumulation of goods at the expense of robbing God is futile. It won't help a man get ahead financially. So the prophet gave them an alternative plan, something to get the people thinking about obedience.

Twice in this sermon, Haggai says to the people, "Consider your ways." In other words, "Think about what you're doing. Are you really further ahead since you've been stealing from God?" I've learned that, as a pastor, I can't really do anything to change a person's giving habits. Everybody makes their own choices. All I can do is challenge people to consider their ways. Life is moving quickly, and many of us need to stop and take inventory about what is important. We need to ask God to help us evaluate our plans in order to honor Him with our finances.

Notice the prophet also says that after a man has considered his ways, he should "'go up to the mountains and bring wood and build the temple, that I may take pleasure in it and be glorified,' says the LORD" (v. 8). In other words, God doesn't want people sitting around and considering their ways forever. He also wants them to take action! If a person knows what is right, he ought to do it. For example, each year my wife and I sit down and determine together how we are going to increase the things we are giving to God. We make a commitment, determine a plan, and take steps to obey the Lord's leading. We don't just talk about it. After we "consider our ways," we have to do something tangible.

The Encouragement

Look at the way Haggai ends his sermon: "Then Haggai, the Lord's messenger, spoke the Lord's message to the people, saying, 'I am with you, says the LORD.' So the LORD stirred up the spirit of Zerubbabel the son of Shealtiel, governor of Judah, and the spirit of Joshua the son of Jehozadak, the high priest, and the spirit of all the remnant of the people; and they came and worked on the house of the LORD of hosts, their God" (vv. 13-14). I love that verse, because it reminds me that God always responds when we take action. His presence is always available for us. When we start to wonder how we'll be able to start tithing, His presence is there to offer encouragement. The Lord is with us, and He'll help us as we obey Him.

Not only is His **presence** with us, but His **power** is also with us. Haggai tells us that the Lord stirred up His people to get them to fulfill their commitment to rebuild the Temple. God gave them the enthusiasm and excitement to do what they had committed themselves to do. I've found that feeling often follows action. Instead of waiting for my feelings to come along before obeying, I have found in my life that if I'll obey, the feelings will eventually follow. If I waited for the feelings, a lot of things would never get done! Many of the disciplines in my life are things I don't feel good about until I do them.

If a believer will take a step of faith and make a commitment to

God, the Lord will be with him and empower him. The Lord will stir his heart, as He stirred the hearts of the people in Haggai's time. What a great encouragement it is to know that God will be with me if I'll obey Him.

Christian, we cannot neglect God. We cannot take His place in order to serve ourselves. In the words of Jesus, "Seek first the kingdom of God and His righteousness, and all these things shall be added to you" (Matthew 6:33). By putting God first, we reprioritize everything else in our lives. It causes us to see things from a new perspective. It puts us on the side of God. But when we put ourselves first, we lose the joy that comes from obedience. As we allow the Spirit of God to confront our lives and help us make a commitment to Him, we'll start to sense His presence and see His power at work in us.

APPLICATION   H A G G A I   1 : 1 - 1 1

1. As you peruse Haggai chapter 1, what was the big problem?

What excuse did the people have for not giving to God?

Have you ever found yourself using that excuse? What is the result of not surrendering to God what is due Him?

What message did the Lord have for His people?

Why is it so easy for us to neglect God and take care of ourselves?

When have you found yourself withholding from the Lord in order to serve your own needs?

What did you do to change the situation?

What was the result of your action?

What do the following passages of Scripture have to say about the amount of money we give to God:

Mark 12:41-44

Luke 16:10

Acts 2:44-45

Acts 4:32

Romans 15:25-27

2 Corinthians 8:2-3

2 Corinthians 9:5

What do Luke 6:38 and Philippians 4:19 have to say about God's supply of resources?

What do Matthew 6:19 and 2 Corinthians 6:9 reveal about giving and eternity?

How can we put these passages into practice? What changes should they render in our lives?

From your perspective, what benefit does a person accrue from establishing a regular pattern of giving?

What effect does regular giving have, according to Galatians 6:6-10?

As you "consider your ways," what are the things you would most like to accomplish in your life?

What are the things you want to have?

What are the things you want to be?

Who are the people or groups you most want to help?

The Books of Ezra and Nehemiah describe in detail the rebuilding of the Temple and the city of Jerusalem. As a matter of fact, Nehemiah even records the names of the people who helped and the very section of the wall each person worked on. Their sacrifice became a memorial to them, to the point that each individual became part of the biblical record!

GIVERS AND TAKERS

GENESIS 13-19

S ome people want to give things away, while others seem bent on taking things for themselves. The Book of Genesis offers a study in contrast between Abraham, a man known for his generosity, and Lot, a man who wanted everything he could get his hands on.

   I. Lot Became Interested in the Wrong Direction
  II. Lot Became Insensitive to God's Voice
 III. Lot Became Incompatible with Himself
  IV. Lot Became Inevitably Involved in Sin
   V. Abraham Gave Away What He Had
  VI. Abraham Gained Position at Home
 VII. Abraham Gained a New Prosperity for His Family

It is more blessed to give than to receive." Remember hearing that when you were a child? Unfortunately, it was usually quoted when you were disappointed about having given away something greater than you received. The word *blessed* in Greek can actually be translated "happy" or "joyful," and the Bible teaches that we will know true joy when we learn what it means to give. Of course, the world sometimes seems to be divided into "givers" and "takers." Some people always seem to be giving away their time and treasures, and some are always looking for something more. I have long been interested in that phenomenon and have enjoyed studying the contrasts between givers and takers in Scripture; for example, the contrast between Mary and Judas that we looked at earlier, and that between Barnabas and Ananias. It seems as though the Lord wants to be certain we understand that it is better to give than to receive, even though the idea appears to go against our very nature.

Consider, for example, the character of Lot. Here was a man who had every opportunity to be a giver but always remained a taker. He came out of the land of Ur with his Uncle Abraham, and through no merit of his own was allowed the opportunity to become wealthy. He had camels and flocks and herds, manservants and maidservants and much wealth, but when faced with the decision of giving or taking, Lot chose to become a taker. It's not a pretty story. Lot decided not to stay with Abraham and work out a plan to share their goods and wealth, but instead chose to strike out on his own in hopes of gaining more wealth for himself. The record of his downfall is given to us in the Book of Genesis, as he gradually deteriorated from a spiritual man into a selfish drunkard. The contrast between Lot and Abraham is a clear picture of the difference between a giver and a taker.

Lot Became Interested in the Wrong Direction

The first thing we note about Lot is that, when given the opportunity, he looked in the wrong direction. It always seems that when we take our eyes off the Lord and become enamored with ourselves, it leads to trouble. In Genesis 13, Lot was given a choice between staying close to Abraham or setting out on his own. Abraham, in his generosity, actually allowed the young man to choose which land he would take. As Lot looked around, he noticed the plains of Jordan were lush and well watered, so he forgot his uncle's generosity and chose that land for himself. The Bible says he decided to pitch his tent close to the city of Sodom.

The city of Sodom has long been used to denote evil and debased practices. We get our word "sodomy" from this city, and Genesis 13:13 notes that "the men of Sodom were exceedingly wicked and sinful against the LORD." Second Peter 2:7-8 describes these people by speaking of "the filthy conduct of the wicked." Jude 7 notes that Sodom was such an evil city that it was "set forth as an example, suffering the vengeance of eternal fire." It was a vile place, yet Lot chose to live there. Even though he had been given all sorts of wonderful opportunities, he became enamored with Sodom, and settled into life among the wicked. This was the first step in his downfall.

I find that becoming comfortable with sin is often the first step in a long, downhill slide. As we walk with God, we'll notice something that looks good. It sounds like fun, it entices us, and pretty soon we've taken our eyes off eternal things and become enamored with the things of this world.

Lot Became Insensitive to God's Voice

The second thing we notice about Lot is that he started listening to the wrong voice. Once we start listening to the world, we have a tendency to tune God out. The Lord still wants to talk with us, but we no longer listen. Lot is a perfect illustration of what happens when a man becomes insensitive to God. For example, after he moved to Sodom, he became involved in the city and wrapped up in its culture. One day the city was attacked and Lot and his family were taken captive. Had it been me instead of Abraham, I might have said, "Serves him right, the greedy boy. He got what's coming to him." But Abraham, godly man that he was, gathered his servants and rescued his nephew. Now it would seem that after being with pagans, captured by enemies, and miraculously delivered by the grace of God and the magnanimous spirit of Abraham, Lot might have stopped to think about life for a minute. He might have taken a moment to wonder, "What am I doing here? How did I ever get involved with people like this?" Instead, he went right back to the city of Sodom. As a matter of fact, the next time he appears, he is the leader of the city!

Later, when Lot is fleeing Sodom and the destruction God has planned for it, he argues with God about where he should go. Here the Lord is trying to save this man's neck, and Lot wants to haggle over the escape route. That just reconfirms something I know to be true: when we start listening to the Siren's song of the world, we stop listening to the voice of God.

Lot Became Incompatible with Himself

Second Peter 2: 6-8 reveals, "And turning the cities of Sodom and Gomorrah into ashes, condemned them to destruction, making them an example to those who afterward would live ungodly; and delivered righteous Lot, who was oppressed with the filthy conduct of the wicked (for that righteous man, dwelling among them, tormented his righteous soul from day to day by seeing and hearing their lawless deeds)." In other words, after Lot started living in that city, thinking it was going to be a wonderful place, he discovered how awful it really was. All around him was unrighteousness. Now, in his heart was a desire to please God, but Lot was always compromising that desire in order to satisfy his tremendous appetite for money. He disliked being among those people but was willing to remain there in order to accumulate more wealth.

Ask yourself a question: Do you think Lot was happy? The Bible says he was oppressed and tormented. He became an unhappy, miserable man because he tried to establish happiness through material wealth rather than spiritual peace.

Lot Became Inevitably Involved in Sin

Lot eventually became an influential man in Sodom, sitting at the gates and judging disputes among people. But it's interesting that when he first went to the area, the Bible says he "pitched his tent toward Sodom." That is, he set up his tent so that when the flap was opened, he could see the city. But it wasn't long before he was living inside it. The next thing you know, he is seated at the gate of it, having become a civic leader. It was inevitable that Lot should become involved in the sin of Sodom.

When the people came after the representatives sent by God, Lot cruelly offered them his daughters to abuse. I can't imagine a man doing anything so awful as to trade one of his children in order to relieve the pressure of a social situation. But Lot hung around wickedness, and in the long run it rubbed off on him. At the end of his life, he is depicted in a cave committing incest with his daughters. How could a man who started out wanting to please God sink so low? It wasn't by one step. Lot took a number of small steps that led him away from the Lord, toward the degradation of his soul. He ended up doing exactly what Sodom was known for—becoming involved in perverse sexual activity. In a drunken stupor, he fathered children by his own daughters. Lot lost everything because he was willing to walk away from God in order to enrich his purse.

Abraham Gave Away What He Had

It's important to keep in mind that Lot didn't really have anything until Abraham gave it to him. Abraham just took his nephew under his wing and got him started in business. Then, when the day came that both men had so many flocks they were competing with each other, Abraham was generous enough to give Lot first choice of the land. Of course, Lot should have insisted his uncle choose first. Instead, he saw his chance to make a killing and grabbed the best land he could find.

Abraham, on the other hand, trusted that God would provide. Throughout his life, Abraham proved that he was a giver. He treated the king of Salem with generosity, was liberal with the son of his bondwoman, and took care of all those who were part of his camp. He gave everything away, and God returned everything to him. When Abraham rejected materialism, he didn't lose. He gained. After Abraham allowed Lot to take the best land, God said to Abraham, "All the land which you see I give to you and your descendants forever" (Genesis 13:15). In giving away what he had, Abraham actually gained more.

Abraham Gained Position at Home

In Genesis 18:19, God said this about Abraham: "For I have known him, in order that he may command his children and his household after him, that they keep the way of the LORD, to do righteousness and justice, that the LORD may bring to Abraham what He has spoken to him." Contrast that with Lot, who ended up in a cave, sexually involved with his own daughters. The fact that Abraham was a giver didn't make him a loser. He gave up temporal things he couldn't keep, and gained eternal things he could never lose.

I have sat with businessmen who sobbed uncontrollably, saddened over the fact that they sacrificed everything for their business success, only to find their success wasn't worth the price they paid. A man I know, who had worked feverishly to achieve material wealth, sat in my office and wept because he had allowed his children to fall into all sorts of evil. "The thing that tears at my heart is that everything they're doing is what I've taught them to do," he told me. "If I could only go back and live my life over!" In becoming a taker, that man lost his position at home.

Abraham Gained a New Prosperity for His Family

The Lord gave back to Abraham everything he had given away. Even the land he had so generously given to his nephew was eventually restored to Abraham. I think the key reason for that can be found in Genesis 13:18: "Then Abram moved his tent, and went and dwelt by the terebinth trees of Mamre, which are in Hebron, and built an altar there to the LORD." Abraham never lost his fellowship with God. He remained close to the Lord, recognizing that his walk with God was more important than the accumulation of wealth. While Lot chased after the unimportant, Abraham followed after the eternal. He kept his family together, protected them from sin, maintained a close walk with God, and gave generously to others. In the end, he didn't lose anything. He got it all back and more.

The world is made up of givers and takers. Lot gained the wealth of Jordan, but lost the companionship of Abraham. He gained a home in Sodom, the city of wickedness, but lost a place near Hebron, whose name means "communion with God." He gained influence in his city, but lost influence in his own home. He gained the friendship of the Sodomites, but lost his fellowship with the Father. God wanted Lot out of that city. He even tried to save Lot's entire family, but they refused to listen to the Lord.

The Bible reveals what happens when a man faces the challenge of materialism. He either becomes a giver or a taker. Wealth is often divisive, drawing men away from God, family, and friends. Those who are takers are ultimately destroyed. Lot put himself first, and the result was his own destruction. But Abraham put God first, and the result was the eternal blessing of God.

1. Where do you see "givers" in our culture?

Who do you know that could be classified as a giver?

How does our culture glorify the "takers"?

In what ways do you see yourself as a giver?

What do you enjoy giving most? To whom?

In what ways do you see yourself as a taker?

As you read Genesis 13, why do you suppose Abraham was so generous to Lot?

What should Lot have done in that situation?

What do you think you would have done?

Why did the city of Sodom entice Lot?

How does hanging around sin make us more susceptible to it?

What can a Christian surrounded by a sinful community do to maintain his or her integrity?

How does giving things away establish a parent as a positive influence in the child's life?

Why do you suppose Lot's sons-in-law failed to listen to him?

How were you influenced by your parents' example?

What have you purchased, thinking it would make you happy, only to find it failed to bring you happiness?

Who is the one person you know who seems most fulfilled and at peace? What part does giving have to do with his or her life?

Take a few moments to pray about becoming a giver. Tell the Lord what you would like to give away and what influence you'd like to have on your world.

Lot's daughters each had a child by him. One child, Moab, became father of the Moabites. The other, Ben-Ammi, became father of the Ammonites. Both tribes were known for their wickedness, and both warred with Israel for centuries. If Lot had never involved himself with Sodom, he would have saved all of Israel much pain and heartache.

GIVING TOO MUCH

When the people of Israel were instructed by God to build the tabernacle, they cheerfully and generously obeyed. This joy-filled example teaches us that God is behind every need and every gift, and He will receive all the glory.

I. God Was Responsible for the Need
II. God Was Responsible for the Giving
III. God Was Responsible for the Offering
IV. God Was Responsible for the Inspiration
V. God Was Responsible for the Glory

Sometimes we can focus on the particulars so much we miss the evident. For example, I heard about a man who was always crossing the border on his bike, with sacks over his shoulder. Each day the border guards would stop and search the sacks, sure that he was a smuggler. But every day they came up empty. The man would take his stuff, stick it back into the sacks, and ride on. The authorities were certain they would one day catch this man carrying smuggled goods across the border on his bicycle, but they never did. Years later, when a border guard ran into the man in a restaurant, he admitted he had been smuggling something valuable: bikes! It was right under their noses every day, and they missed it.

I think stewardship can be that way at times. We talk about tithing, and discuss the aspects of stewardship, and focus on the various instructions in the Scriptures that detail how we should use our resources, but we miss the most important lesson of all: God wants us to give. He expects us to love Him and reflect our love by supporting His work. What we do with our money reveals what we believe in our hearts. That's the most important lesson we can take from any study of stewardship. Of course, there are many great verses that help us to understand that truth, but the most exciting passage of all, in my estimation, occurs in the Book of Exodus. This portion of Scripture shows us how God expects us to be involved with Him in our lives and our giving.

> And Moses spoke to all the congregation of the children of Israel, saying, "This is the thing which the LORD commanded, saying: 'Take from among you an offering to the LORD. Whoever is of a willing heart, let him bring it as an offering to the LORD. . . . All who are gifted artisans among you shall come and make all that the LORD has commanded. . . .'" And all the congregation of the children of Israel departed from the presence of Moses. Then everyone came whose heart was stirred, and everyone whose spirit was willing, and they brought the LORD's offering for the work of the tabernacle of meeting, for all its service, and for the holy garments. They came, both men and women, as many as had a

willing heart, and brought earrings and nose rings, rings and necklaces, all jewelry of gold, that is, every man who made an offering of gold to the LORD. . . . and they spoke to Moses, saying, "The people bring much more than enough for the service of the work which the LORD commanded us to do." So Moses gave a commandment, and they caused it to be proclaimed throughout the camp, saying, "Let neither man nor woman do any more work for the offering of the sanctuary." And the people were restrained from bringing, for the material they had was sufficient for all the work to be done—indeed too much (Exodus 35:4-5, 10, 20-22; 36:5-7).

God Was Responsible for the Need

The people of Israel were incredibly generous in recreating the tabernacle. It has been estimated that to reconstruct the tabernacle today would require more than $10 million. So at that time, the money required to take on such a project must have been absolutely astronomical. Yet God's people, under the leadership of the Holy Spirit, were able to construct it due to their generous giving. In fact, they contributed so much money Moses had to tell them to stop giving. Can you imagine a pastor standing before his flock and saying, "Stop it! We don't need any more!"? It may sound preposterous, but that's exactly what occurred.

The need for the offering was something God had caused. He was responsible for it. Moses didn't think up some idea to build a church; it originated in the heart of God. Moses simply presented the idea to the people, and they in turn responded to the need. The same God who had led them out of slavery, parted the Red Sea, and given them the Promised Land, now desired a meeting place for His people. He wanted Israel to have a place where they could be with Him. His glory would actually reside within that tabernacle. So the Lord caused the need to be made known.

That may sound like a mundane principle, but reflect on it for a moment. Too often when a church is considering financial support, we talk about the needs of men. We discuss the needs of the budget, or the needs of the organization, but if the ministry is of the Lord, the need actually springs from the heart of God. The necessity grows from a God-ordained need. For example, at our church we have a big ministry, and it reaches out through radio, through Christian schools, and through a college campus. We support missionaries who are taking the Gospel to all parts of the globe, representing our church and the Lord Jesus Christ. We have services that reach thousands of people each Sunday. And all these ministries sprang from the heart of God. If He hadn't begun the work by placing His vision in the hearts of men, none of this would have succeeded. I don't like to hear people talk about how "we've got to give because the church needs money," because the problems of ministry do not spring from people. If you want to blame someone for a ministry's financial needs, you had best blame God, for He is the one who gave men and women the vision. All they did was respond to His call in faith.

The people of Israel needed to give money to construct a tabernacle because God got an idea. He told the people it was their responsibility to meet the challenge, and they took it from there.

God Was Responsible for the Giving

Remember, the giving potential of every person in Israel was arranged by God. Even though they had been in slavery, the Lord arranged for them to have $10 million worth of gold! He had it all worked out; all the people had to do was obey. God arranged for the Egyptians to give the Jews going-away gifts as they left Egypt which became known as the "plunder of Egypt." So the tabernacle of Israel was actually built with Egyptian gold. It's amazing how God worked out all the details to take care of the need. The Egyptians literally gave Israel enough money to construct their worship center.

One of the overwhelming facts about this whole story is that God had worked out all the details long before the need existed. He arranged for the need to be met at exactly the right time. There was no plea on the part of the Jews. They didn't ask their unbelieving neighbors to buy a brick for their building. They just waited for God to bring them the resources, and those resources were generously turned over to the Lord when it was time for construction.

The fact is, some people working through this Bible study may be thinking about starting to tithe, but they're worried because they don't know where the money will come from. My answer to that is simple: We may not know, but God does. He's already got it all worked out. It's going to be some creative thing we haven't even thought of, but God has already put it together. He has put the pieces into place, and now He is waiting to release them through our response of faith. As soon as we begin to give, He will provide for the need.

God Was Responsible for the Offering

The offering made for the tabernacle was God-given. The people carried out the details of this offering according to the exact commandments of the Lord. For example, God told them it was to be a free-will offering. In Exodus 35:5 He said that the offering was to be from whoever was "of a willing heart." Verse 21 explains that the gifts were made from those whose hearts were stirred, whom the Holy Spirit made willing. This offering was an expression of love from the hearts of the people, which was exactly what God intended. There wasn't any coercion or motivational program. There was no direct mail, no high-powered speaker, just a God-ordained free-will offering.

It was also a revelational offering. That is, the people didn't have any doubt what they were supposed to give, for God had told each of them exactly what to do. That's why Moses told the people that they should bring "all that the LORD had commanded" (v. 10). That is the reason we all must pray before offering a gift to the Lord. We ought to ask Him specifically what we should give, and He'll tell us. I sometimes think the reason people don't know what to give God is because they've never asked Him what to give. We don't know what to do because we've never come in faith and said, "Lord, here is my income, and here are my stewardship opportunities. What do you want me to give?" God is anxious to share with us if we will just come and ask Him. Usually He does it through His Word, and sometimes He does it during times of prayer, but He is always willing to tell us.

God was responsible for this offering. Not only did He make it a free-will offering and a revelational offering, but He made it an offering specifically to God, not to some organization promising to use the money in a particular way. Verse 5 makes a point of calling this "an offering to the LORD." So do verses 21, 22, and 29. These gifts weren't given to a building fund or to strengthen the economy of Israel. The people knew their offerings were going straight to God. Imagine how different our feelings about giving would be if we understood that our gifts were going directly to God!

Sometimes people try to use their gifts to manipulate others. They get upset with a church decision and withhold their gifts, or they don't like something the pastor says so they put all their money into some special fund. But when we make an offering, it isn't going to one fund or another—it's going to God. We ought to be willing to allow God to use that money as He sees fit.

When the people of Israel came with their gifts, God made sure it was an inclusive offering. The Bible clearly points out that Moses invited everyone to participate—men and women, young and old, as many as were willing. Everybody got involved with giving. That's how a church ought to function. Singles should participate just as married couples do. Families should take part in the same way as those whose children are grown. Teenagers can do their part, just like senior citizens. I really believe a church can never be all God wants it to be until every group and subsection participates with the Lord in giving. It's easy for a college student to say, "God doesn't expect anything from me; the older people will have to pay the bills." But the Lord looks to every individual to give what they are called to give. A person may not have much money, but God isn't expecting that person to fund everything that goes on in church. The Lord is simply expecting that person to take part and to contribute a portion of his income as a reflection of his love for God. The Lord will lay on each individual's heart what he or she should give. Nobody is excluded from giving, because God doesn't want anyone excluded from the blessing. No matter what your financial state, if you got your money from the Lord, it belongs to Him, so you ought to give.

God Was Responsible for the Inspiration

As you read through Exodus 35 and 36, you find one consistent pattern: People gave enthusiastically because God had taken control of their hearts. These people couldn't wait to get involved in giving. They didn't give reluctantly or drag their feet to the worship service. They were excited about what God was doing in their midst. When we get His perspective on things, and see how our investment is making a difference for eternity, we can experience that same God-inspired excitement.

The Bible is clear that when we do God's work God's way,

participating out of love and thankfulness, there will be enough money. As a matter of fact, my favorite verse in this entire story is Exodus 36:5, when the craftsmen who were building the tabernacle showed up to tell Moses, "The people have brought more than enough! Tell them to stop!"

Too often a church or ministry has great vision but limited resources. The leaders have a vision from the Lord for reaching their world with the love of Jesus Christ, but for some reason there is a problem getting others to participate with them in implementing the vision. At most churches, less than 50% of the members tithe. How in the world can a church implement a vision unless the people choose to become part of it? I firmly believe that if every Christian were to tithe to his church, we would see unprecedented growth and ministry occur in this country. People want an uncommon church, but they offer a common commitment. And an uncommon church cannot function unless it is supported with an uncommon commitment of resources.

God Was Responsible for the Glory

The results of that offering in Exodus brought tremendous glory to God. After that offering, He had a house—the tabernacle, a beautiful and portable dwelling place for the Lord. The Jews carried that with them wherever they went. I would love to have been there for the first worship service, with all the excitement of the new structure. I used to pastor a church that met in a mobile home, and I'll never forget the day we moved out of that cramped little space into our new building. It was a glorious day, for we all realized God had done a tremendous work in our midst, growing us from a few families in a Bible study to a strong, healthy body of believers. Eventually we outgrew that new building and had to create a new sanctuary, and again we marched out of our small building and into a wonderful new structure that had been built with the generous offerings of the people. Everything the people had invested was worth it. They were able to see their faith become a reality, and the result was that God was glorified.

When the people of Israel gave to build the tabernacle, God had a home, and the people had a hope. Throughout their years of wandering in the wilderness, the Lord's presence was with them. The tabernacle stayed with them in the wilderness, reminding them of the importance of remaining close to God. Because they had given sacrificially, God was glorified.

There is one last thing we need to consider. God got a home, the people got hope, and we got a great story of God's faithfulness. Exodus 35 & 36 is a true story of people who dared to believe in God, and it should build our own faith as we consider how we ought to give. God loves us to give cheerfully and wants us to give out of love. Giving is an act of worship unto the Lord, and when we enthusiastically follow the principles in His Word, we can experience a tremendous blessing. God will be glorified and His work will be accomplished on earth because we made a commitment to sacrificially give to Him. That is the commitment He seeks from each of us.

APPLICATION   E X O D U S   3 5   &   3 6

---

1. Look through the example of giving in Exodus 35 and 36. What motivated the people to give so generously?

    In what way could it be said that God was responsible for the giving?

In light of this story, how would you respond to someone who claimed, "Those guys are always asking for money!"

How is God behind the needs of ministry?

Does God tell us what to give? How?

To what has God instructed you to give?

Have you ever heard of another instance in which people gave too much? What was the occasion?

What motivates you to give generously?

What do you think would happen if everybody in your church started tithing?

What principles for handling your money do you find in chapters 10 and 11 of the Book of Proverbs?

In chapter 10, what do verses 2, 4, 5, 6, 7, 9, and 22 reveal about our perspective of money?

In chapter 11, what do verses 4, 17, and 24-28 reveal about our use of money?

In Proverbs 13, 14, and 15 there are several helpful guidelines for handling finances. Read Proverbs 13: 4, 7, 11, and 22. How would you summarize Solomon's advice to his son?

Read Proverbs 14:14, 26, and 31. What promises are we offered regarding our use of our resources?

What do you find in Proverbs 15: 6, 16, 17, and 27, regarding our attitude toward wealth?

6. What other guidelines for handling money do you find in the following passages:

   Proverbs 16:3, 33

   Proverbs 17:3, 16

   Proverbs 19:17

   Proverbs 21:25-26

   Proverbs 22:1, 2, 4, 9

7. What has been the most helpful thing you've learned from this study?

What is one commitment you have made because of this study?

DID YOU KNOW

King Solomon was probably the wealthiest man in the history of the world. His holdings and income were greater than any king before or since. Yet at the end of his life, Solomon wrote these words: "He who loves silver will not be satisfied with silver; nor he who loves abundance, with increase" (Ecclesiastes 5:10). King Solomon understood that the accumulation of wealth means nothing if we do not have a close relationship with God.

Turning Point
Resource Books
By Dr. David Jeremiah

What the Bible Says About Angels
Dr. Jeremiah goes straight to God's Word to deliver
fascinating insights about angels, God's majestic messen-
gers. You'll learn that the Bible's rich teaching on angels
is not a trivial fad but a fascinating doorway into sound,
life-giving, spiritual truth that will help you draw closer
than ever to the God you serve.
ANGHBK (Hardback) $19
ANGSG (Study Guide) $9

Prayer—The Great Adventure
Dr. David Jeremiah explores "the Lord's Prayer"
which Jesus gave to His disciples and explains how you
can put that pattern into practice in your own life. As you
study this prayer and begin to implement our Lord's
teaching, you'll become more thankful for what He has
done and begin to see His power at work.
PGAHBK (Hard Cover Book) $19
PGASG (Study Guide) $9

Escape the Coming Night:
The Bright Hope of Revelation
Let Dr. David Jeremiah be your guide through
the terrifying heights and unfathomable depths of the
Book of Revelation. Arm yourself with prophetic truth
about things to come so you can live every moment
for God, because the end is so near.
REVBK $13
REVSGP (Study Guide pkg., 4 volumes) $28

The Handwriting on the Wall:
Secrets from the Prophecies of Daniel
Daniel, divinely inspired, accurately prophesied the rise
and fall of empires and their rulers. We cannot pass Daniel
off as just the man in the lion's den or the "dreamer." To
know Daniel is to know how to live today and look
into the future with confidence.
HOWBK $12
HOWSGP (Study Guide pkg., 3 volumes) $22

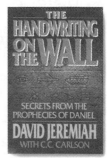

ORDER 1-800-947-1993

OTHER STUDY GUIDES & BOOKS
AVAILABLE THROUGH TURNING POINT

Audio cassette albums are also available. For information use our toll-free number.

SELECTION	CODE	QTY	PRICE	TOTAL
STUDY GUIDES				
Escape the Coming Night (Revelation, 4 volume package)	REVSGP	____	$ 28	$ ____
The Power of Encouragement	POESG	____	$ 9	____
For Such a Time As This—The Book of Esther	ESTSG	____	$ 9	____
Ten Burning Questions from Psalms	TBQSG	____	$ 9	____
Knowing the God You Worship	KGWSG	____	$ 9	____
Seeking Wisdom—Finding Gold	WISSG	____	$ 9	____
The Handwriting on the Wall (Daniel, 3 volume package)	HOWSGP	____	$ 22	____
Invasion of Other Gods (New Age)	IOGSG	____	$ 9	____
Worship	WORSG	____	$ 9	____
Turning Toward Integrity (James)	TTIBK	____	$ 10	____
Turning Toward Joy (Philippians)	TTJBK	____	$ 10	____
The Power of Love (1 Corinthians 13)	POLSG	____	$ 9	____
Spiritual Warfare (Ephesians 6)	SPWSG	____	$ 9	____
The Fruit of the Spirit (Galatians 5:16-26)	FOSSG	____	$ 9	____
Home Improvement	HMISG	____	$ 9	____
What the Bible Says About Angels	ANGSG	____	$ 9	____
Greatest Stories Ever Told (Parables)	GSTSG	____	$ 9	____
A Nation in Crisis (Joshua, Volume 1)	NICSG1	____	$ 9	____
A Nation in Crisis (Joshua, Volume 2)	NICSG2	____	$ 9	____
When Wisdom Turns to Foolishness (Solomon)	WTFSG	____	$ 9	____
Signs of the Second Coming (Matthew 24 & 25)	SSCSG	____	$ 9	____
Core Values of the Church (1 Corinthians, 3 volume pkg.)	CVCSGP	____	$ 22	____
How to Be Happy According to Jesus (Beatitudes)	HTHSG	____	$ 9	____
God Meant It for Good (Life of Joseph, 2 volume pkg.)	JOSSGP	____	$ 18	____
Christ's Death and Resurrection	CDRSGP	____	$ 9	____
Overcoming Loneliness	OCLSG	____	$ 9	____
Prayer—The Great Adventure	PGASG	____	$ 9	____
BOOKS				
The Handwriting on the Wall (Daniel)	HOWBK	____	$ 12	____
Escape the Coming Night (Revelation)	REVBK	____	$ 13	____
The Power of Encouragement	POEBK	____	$ 13	____
Overcoming Loneliness	OCLBK	____	$ 10	____
Invasion of Other Gods (New Age)	IOGBK	____	$ 13	____
What the Bible Says About Angels	ANGHBK	____	$ 19	____
Prayer—The Great Adventure	PGAHBK	____	$ 19	____

For information and Discover, Visa, or MasterCard orders call:

1-800-947-1993

POSTAGE AND HANDLING CHART

For Orders	Add
Up to $5.99	$1.50
$6.00-$19.99	$2.50
$20.00-$50.99	$3.50
$51.00-$99.99	$6.00
$100.00 & over	$9.00

MERCHANDISE TOTAL	____
SHIPPING/HANDLING	____
SUBTOTAL	____
CA RESIDENTS ONLY ADD 7.25% TAX	____
GIFT TO MINISTRY	____
TOTAL	$ ____

Please enclose payment with order. Make check or money order payable to:

TURNING POINT • P.O. Box 3838 • San Diego, CA 92163-1838 *(Please allow 4-6 weeks for delivery)*

Mr/Mrs/Miss _____

Address _____

City/State/Zip _____

I listen to *Turning Point* on (station call letters): _____ Phone _____